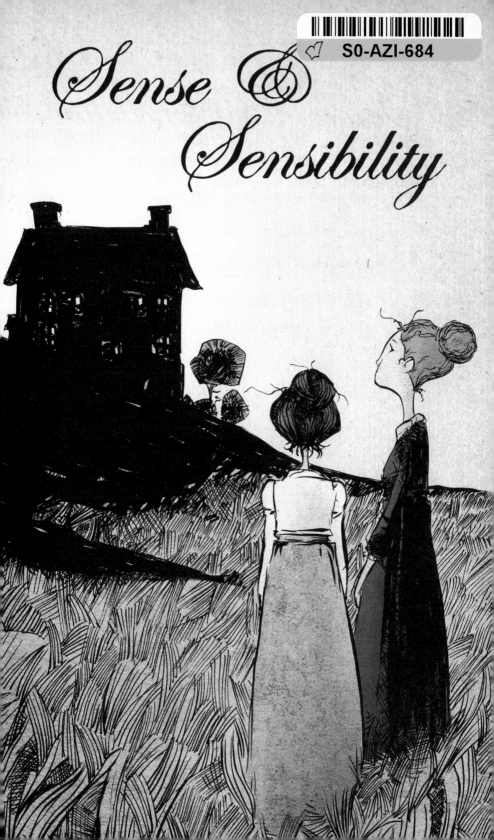

Sense & Sensibility

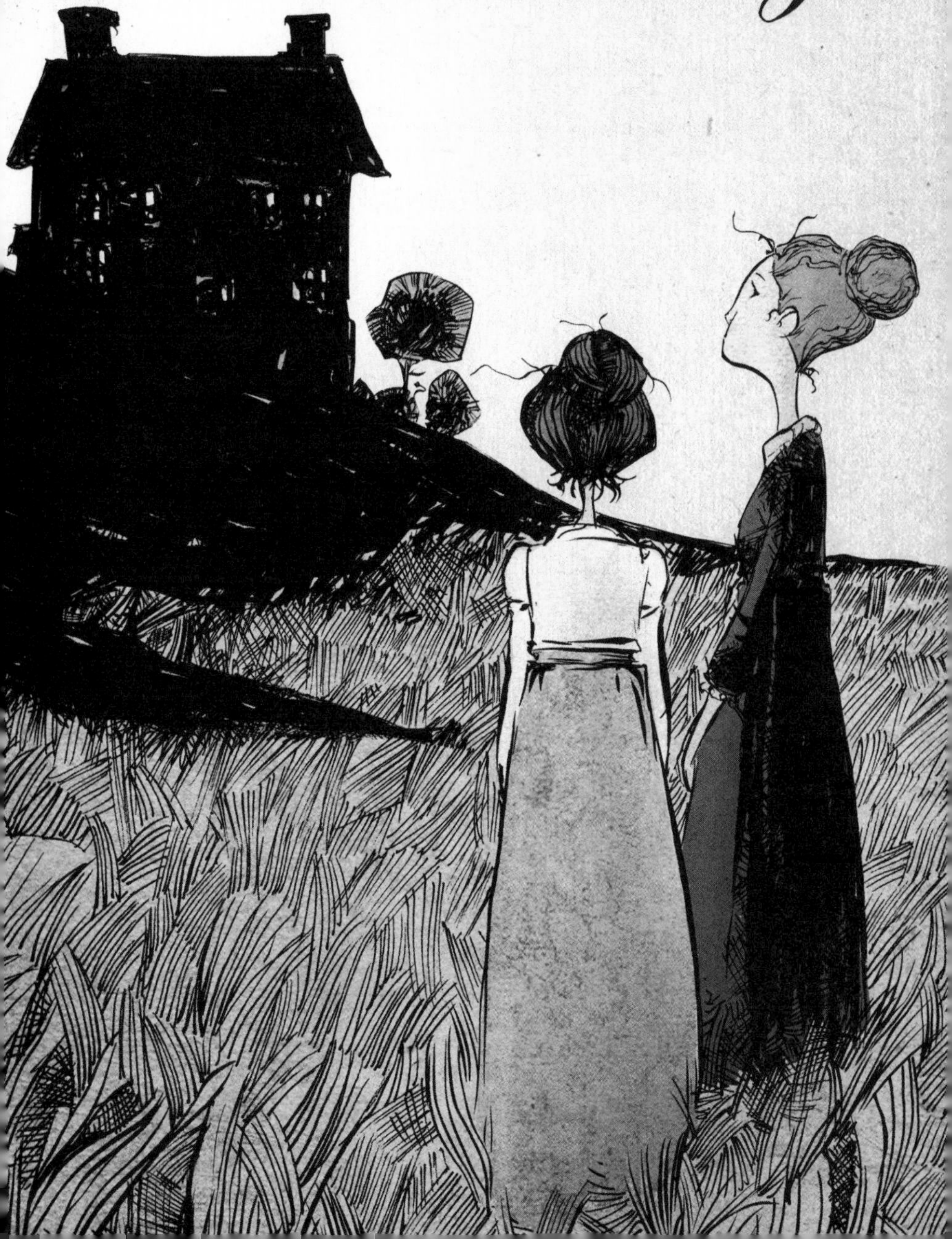

Sense & Sensibility

Adapted from the novel by
Jane Austen

Writer	Nancy Butler
Artist	Sonny Liew
Colorist	SotoColor's L. Molinar
Letterer	VC's Joe Sabino
Cover Artists	Sonny Liew & Skottie Young
Assistant Editor	Michael Horwitz
Editor	Nate Cosby
Senior Editor	Ralph Macchio
Collection Editor	Mark D. Beazley
Editorial Assistants	James Emmett & Joe Hochstein
Assistant Editors	Nelson Ribeiro & Alex Starbuck
Editor, Special Projects	Jennifer Grünwald
Senior Editor, Special Projects	Jeff Youngquist
Senior Vice President of Sales	David Gabriel
Production	Jerry Kalinowski
Book Design	Arlene So
Editor in Chief	Joe Quesada
Publisher	Dan Buckley
Executive Producer	Alan Fine

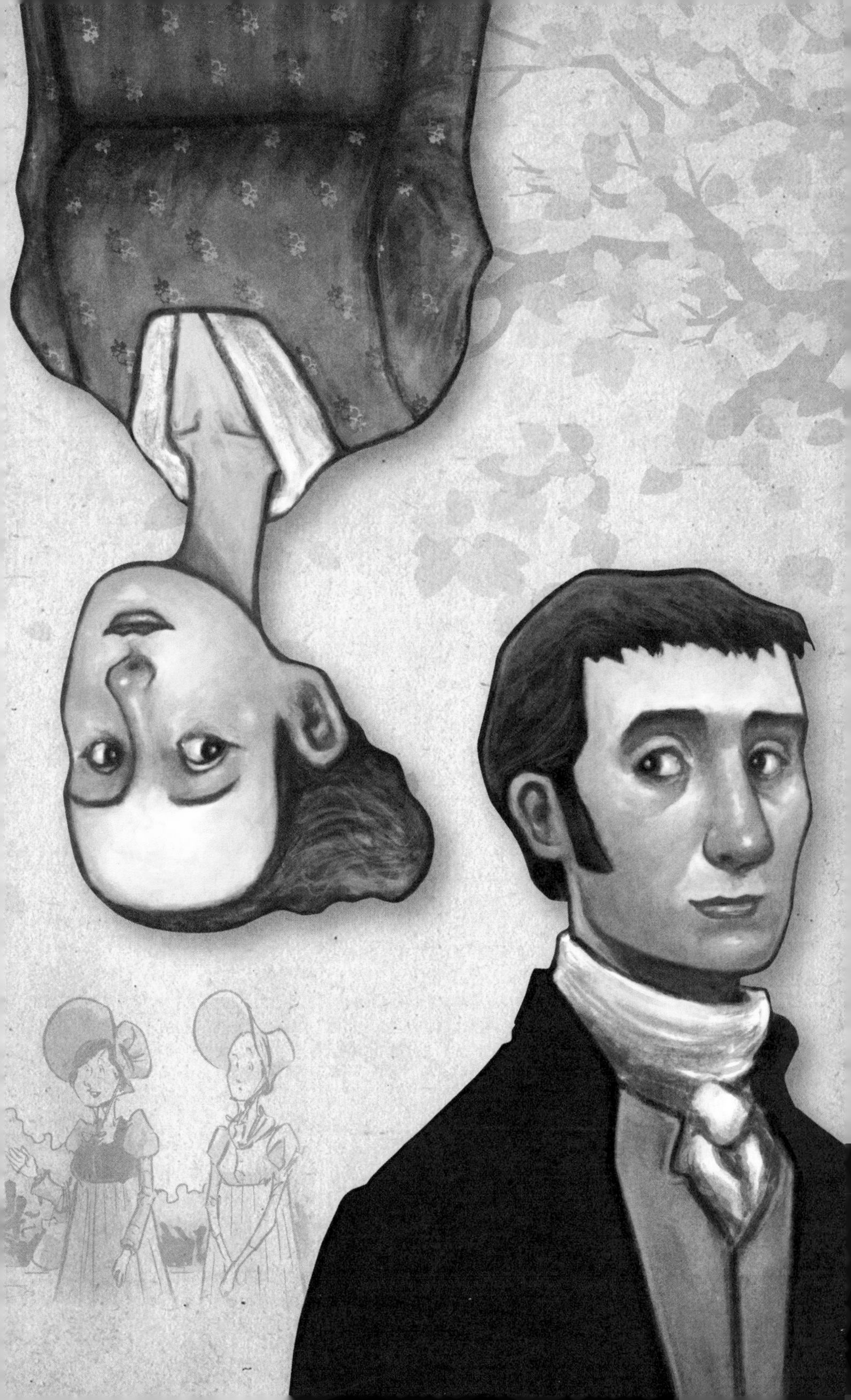

Sense & Sensibility

Jane Austen continues to mystify.

Since 1883, her books have never been out of print, and there is an ever-escalating subgenre of romance and mystery fiction based on characters she created. There is even a series in which Jane herself is a crime-solving detective. In the Huffington Post's 2010 poll of the best romance novels, Austen came in at numbers 1 and 3, for *Pride and Prejudice* and *Sense and Sensibility*, respectively. And let's not forget the slew of Hollywood, Bollywood, and BBC film productions based on her work. Not too shabby for an author who died nearly two hundred years ago.

Yet Austen never set out to become a renowned author, one adored by readers and analyzed by scholars. She initially wrote stories as entertainment for her large family, using her sharp observational skills and quick wit to bring her characters to life. When her books *were* published—the first was *Sense and Sensibility* in 1811—she didn't even use her own name and so was never acclaimed in her lifetime.

So what accounts for the enduring popularity of these stories where nothing happens on a grand scale, where characters engage in endless small talk and the protagonists suffer in silence and only reveal their true feelings at the very end of the tale?

Sense and Sensibility is a good place to look for some answers. Arguably the most complex of Austen's stories, it introduces us to one of her favorite themes — family dynamics. As has been pointed out by analysts of the book, this is not so much a romance as it is the story of the love of two sisters. Two very different sisters, I might add. The emotionally volatile Marianne and the outwardly serene Elinor couldn't be more polar opposites, yet Austen never takes sides; she makes readers care for them equally. She also makes you want to shake both of them frequently — to tell Elinor to loosen up and to scold Marianne for being such a drama queen. Yet no matter how infuriating they can be, we are ultimately engaged by the unflagging affection they have for each other. This was Austen's chief aim — portraying characters with all their flaws and foibles exposed and expecting us to cherish them in spite of it.

It is also in this book that Austen first tackles the British inheritance laws that outraged her sense of fairness, and she openly champions the women who were at the mercy of husbands, fathers and brothers who controlled all the money. No well-bred Regency lady, including Austen herself, was expected to toil for a living and as a result many single women and widows were dependent on the good will of male relations. So even though Austen makes John Dashwood an amusing buffoon, not far beneath the surface lurks a simmering resentment at this pompous fool — and his grasping wife — who beggared his stepmother and her daughters. Austen clearly has a personal bone to pick…and she picks it clean.

When Marvel asked me to adapt *Sense and Sensibility* (after the very gratifying success of their *Pride and Prejudice*, ahem…) I couldn't wait to get started. But while re-reading the book, I realized I was in for some rough going. Austen had originally written *Elinor and Marianne* as an epistolary novel, in the form of letters. Although she eventually changed the format, many key scenes are still conveyed through narrative rather than dialogue. Not the optimum source material for a graphic novel, let me tell you. So I hope readers will forgive me for taking some liberties — in the creation of speeches where none existed and the fleshing out of scenes Austen merely hints at in the book…including Edward's proposal to Elinor, which just *had* to take place on the page!

In every other respect, I believe I stayed faithful to the letter of the book. And that I properly captured those heightened moments of revelation — Brandon's halting tale of the two Elizas, Elinor's confession of her despair over Edward's secret engagement, Willoughby's penitence, Marianne's vows to reform, and Edward's admission of his feelings for Elinor — that readers hold dear. For all her cool, observational eye, Austen knew how to tug at the heartstrings…and I never forgot that.

Artist Sonny Liew's contribution to this project was really the icing on the cake. His lyrical illustration style was a perfect fit for a Regency-era story, and his playful use of chibi figures to enhance Austen's humorous scenes was inspired. In the true spirit of collaboration, Sonny and I bounced ideas and insights off each other throughout the entire process, and I think the book is better for it.

Now, reader, I invite you to turn the page and enter the world of the Dashwood family, a place where I have most happily dwelled these past eight months.

—Nancy Butler

Nancy Butler adapted the New York Times *bestselling graphic novel* Pride and Prejudice *for Marvel Illustrated. She is the author of 12 Signet Regencies and three Signet Christmas novellas. Butler was twice awarded the RITA by the Romance Writers of America, won two Reviewer's Choice Awards from* Romantic Times Magazine, *and was retired to the Hall of Fame by the New Jersey Romance Writers after winning four Golden Leaf Awards. Under her own name, Nancy Hajeski, she is also the author of young adult nonfiction, including the* Hammond Book of Presidents, Hammond Undercover: Princesses, Undercover: Rocks and Minerals, *and* Undercover: Sharks.

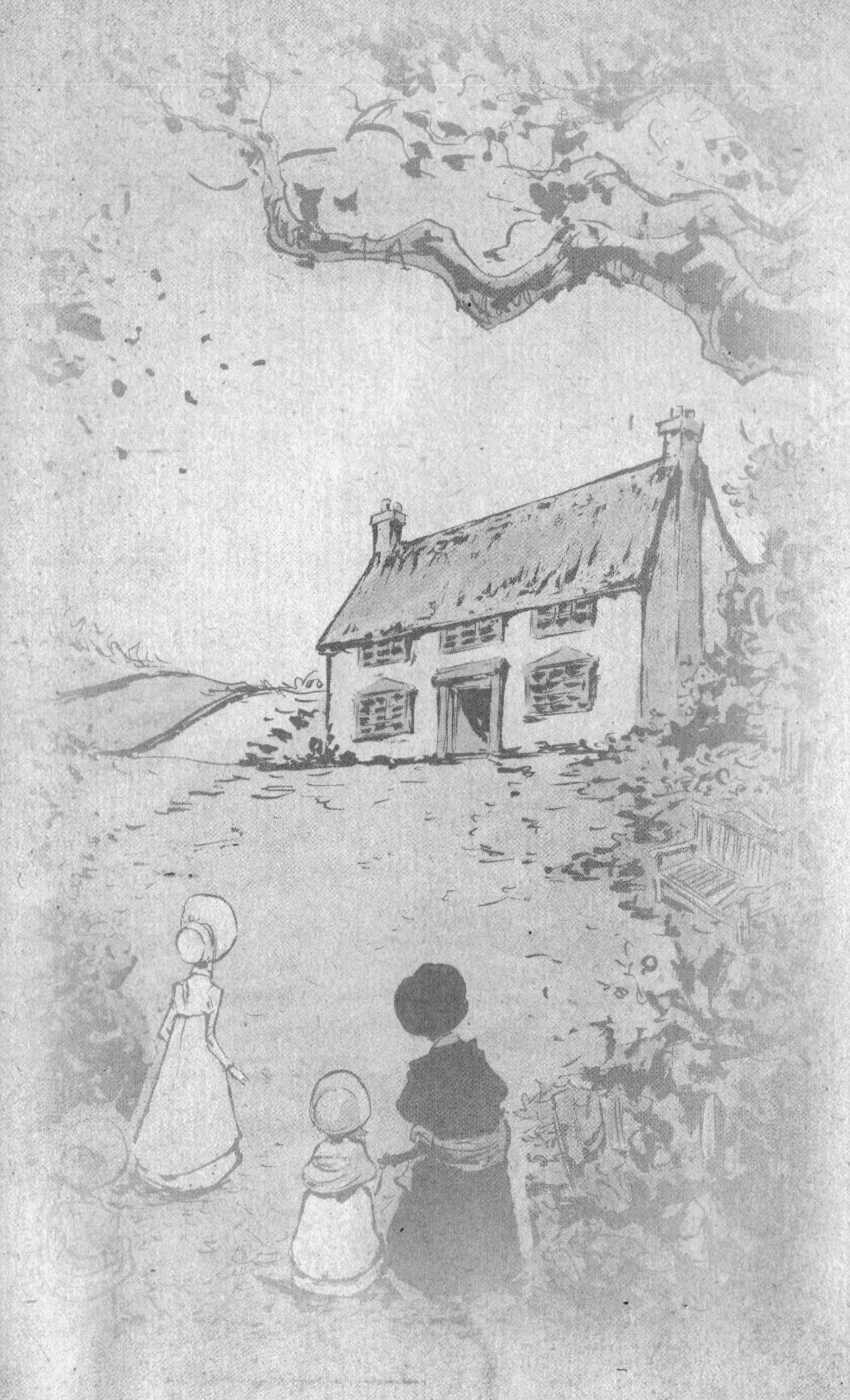

THE DASHWOOD FAMILY HAD LONG BEEN SETTLED IN SUSSEX AT THEIR RESIDENCE, NORLAND PARK.

WHEN THE PREVIOUS DASHWOOD TENANT, A SINGLE GENTLEMAN OF ADVANCED YEARS, LOST HIS SISTER, HE INVITED HIS NEPHEW, HENRY, TO LIVE WITH HIM AND KEEP HIM COMPANY.

HENRY WAS THE FATHER OF ONE SON BY HIS FIRST WIFE, AND OF THREE DAUGHTERS BY HIS PRESENT LADY--ELINOR, MARIANNE, AND MARGARET.

THE SON, JOHN, HAD BEEN AMPLY PROVIDED FOR BY HIS LATE MOTHER, AND FURTHER INCREASED HIS HOLDINGS BY A PRUDENT MARRIAGE.

YET IT WAS TO JOHN'S YOUNG SON THAT THE OLD GENTLEMAN LEFT HIS FORTUNE WHEN HE DIED, LEAVING HENRY THE PROPERTY AND BEQUEATHING HIS THREE GIRLS A MERE THOUSAND POUNDS EACH.

HENRY HAD EXPECTED TO LIVE MANY MORE YEARS, PUTTING ASIDE THE INCOME FROM THE ESTATE AS A LEGACY FOR HIS FAMILY.

ALAS, ONLY A YEAR LATER...

YOU MUST REMEMBER YOUR PROMISE TO LOOK AFTER YOUR SISTERS AND THEIR MOTHER, JOHN.

MY G-GREAT REGRET...IS THAT I HAVE B-BARELY TEN THOUSAND POUNDS TO LEAVE THEM.

YOU MAY REST EASY, FATHER. I WILL DO EVERYTHING IN MY POWER TO MAKE SURE THEY ARE...

COMFORTABLE.

MRS. JOHN DASHWOOD ARRIVED AT NORLAND THE DAY AFTER HENRY'S FUNERAL.

JUST LOOK AT THE STATE OF THE WAINSCOTING.

THE HOUSE IS SADLY IN NEED OF REFURBISHING...

SHE SENT NO WORD, NO WARNING. AND MY POOR HENRY BARELY ONE DAY IN HIS GRAVE.

THIS IS INDELICATE IN THE EXTREME, ELINOR.

I VOW I WILL QUIT THIS HOUSE TODAY RATHER THAN WATCH HER QUEENING IT OVER US ALL.

IT IS HER HOUSE NOW.

BUT PLEASE THINK A MOMENT, MAMA. LEAVING WOULD BE MOST IMPROPER. AND WHERE WOULD WE GO?

I WILL STAY, FOR YOU AND YOUR SISTERS' SAKE. I WOULD NOT WISH TO CREATE A BREACH WITH YOUR BROTHER.

AH, BUT I CANNOT LIKE HIS WIFE.

I FEAR WE MUST ALL GOVERN OUR FEELINGS IN THAT RESPECT.

COME, LET US GREET HER WITH PROPER ATTENTION.

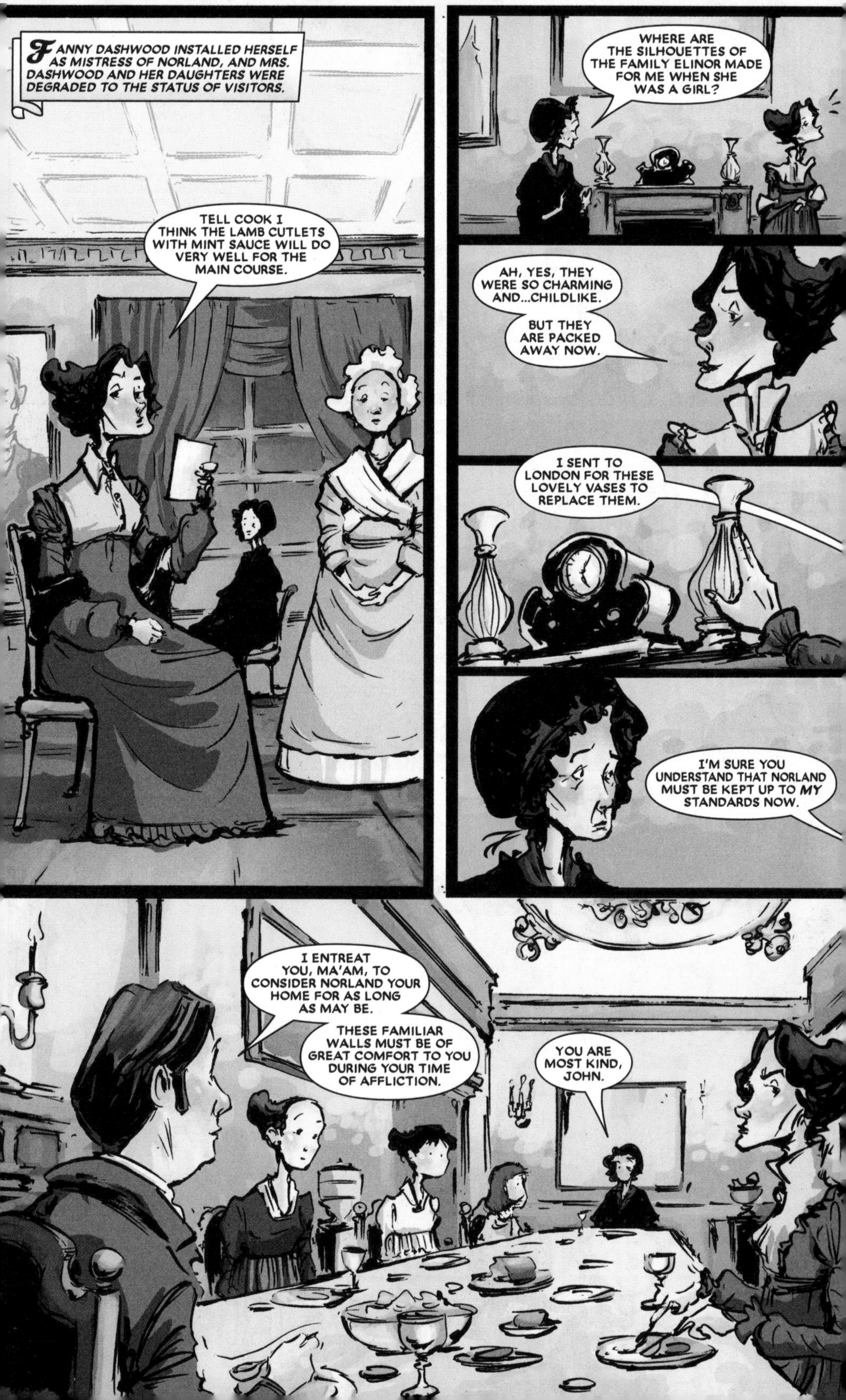
FANNY DASHWOOD INSTALLED HERSELF AS MISTRESS OF NORLAND, AND MRS. DASHWOOD AND HER DAUGHTERS WERE DEGRADED TO THE STATUS OF VISITORS.
TELL COOK I THINK THE LAMB CUTLETS WITH MINT SAUCE WILL DO VERY WELL FOR THE MAIN COURSE.
WHERE ARE THE SILHOUETTES OF THE FAMILY ELINOR MADE FOR ME WHEN SHE WAS A GIRL?
AH, YES, THEY WERE SO CHARMING AND...CHILDLIKE.
BUT THEY ARE PACKED AWAY NOW.
I SENT TO LONDON FOR THESE LOVELY VASES TO REPLACE THEM.
I'M SURE YOU UNDERSTAND THAT NORLAND MUST BE KEPT UP TO *MY* STANDARDS NOW.
I ENTREAT YOU, MA'AM, TO CONSIDER NORLAND YOUR HOME FOR AS LONG AS MAY BE.
THESE FAMILIAR WALLS MUST BE OF GREAT COMFORT TO YOU DURING YOUR TIME OF AFFLICTION.
YOU ARE MOST KIND, JOHN.

I AM RELIEVED THAT JOHN IS NOT EAGER TO SEE US GONE.

I KNOW YOU HAVE BEEN MELANCHOLY AT THE THOUGHT OF LEAVING OUR HOME. IN TRUTH, WE ALL HAVE.

YOU MISTAKE ME. MY SPIRITS HAVE NOW REVIVED AFTER THE LOSS OF YOUR FATHER AND I AM EAGER TO BE AWAY FROM HERE.

I HAVE BEGUN INQUIRING FOR A SUITABLE DWELLING IN THIS NEIGHBORHOOD AND LEARNED ONLY TODAY THAT HARTLEY HALL IS TO LET.

BUT CAN WE AFFORD SUCH A GRAND PLACE? OUR MEANS ARE QUITE LIMITED.

BEFORE HE DIED, YOUR FATHER CONFIDED IN ME THAT JOHN PROMISED TO PROVIDE FOR US. I ADMIT I REPROACHED MYSELF FOR BEING UNJUST, THINKING HIM INCAPABLE OF GENEROSITY.

A LESSER AMOUNT WOULD SUFFICE, BUT A SETTLEMENT OF SEVEN THOUSAND POUNDS OR SO WOULD SUPPORT US IN SOME AFFLUENCE.

*B*UT NOTHING, AS THEY SAY, IS SET IN STONE...

I DON'T BELIEVE I MENTIONED IT, MY LOVE, BUT I INTEND TO SETTLE A THOUSAND POUNDS EACH ON MY SISTERS.

I CANNOT SAY THAT I APPROVE. HOW COULD YOU DEPRIVE YOUR ONLY CHILD OF SUCH A SUM?

BUT IT WAS MY FATHER'S LAST REQUEST...THAT I SHOULD ASSIST HIS WIDOW AND DAUGHTERS.

TEN TO ONE HE WAS LIGHTHEADED AT THE TIME.

HAD HE BEEN IN HIS RIGHT SENSES, HE WOULD NOT HAVE BEGGED YOU TO GIVE HALF YOUR FORTUNE AWAY FROM YOUR CHILD.

IF OUR SON WERE TO MARRY AND HAVE A LARGE BROOD, SUCH A SUM WOULD BE A VERY CONVENIENT ADDITION.

PLUS I MUST BEAR IN MIND THAT THE GIRLS WILL HAVE THREE THOUSAND POUNDS EACH UPON THEIR MOTHER'S DEATH.

AND UNTIL THAT TIME THEY CAN, I DARESAY, LIVE VERY COMFORTABLY ON THE INTEREST.

MONEY ONCE PARTED WITH WILL *NEVER* RETURN.

I DON'T WISH TO DO ANYTHING *MEAN.* PERHAPS FIVE HUNDRED POUNDS EACH...

WHAT BROTHER ON *EARTH* WOULD DO ANYTHING HALF SO MUCH FOR HIS SISTERS, IF EVEN *REALLY* HIS SISTERS?

AS IT IS IN THIS CASE--ONLY HALF BLOOD.

I WONDER IF IT WOULD NOT BE BETTER TO DO SOMETHING FOR THEIR MOTHER WHILE SHE LIVES. SOMETHING OF AN ANNUITY, SAY A HUNDRED POUNDS A YEAR.

BUT WHAT IF SHE LIVES TO A GREAT AGE? IT IS AN UNPLEASANT THING TO HAVE SUCH A DRAIN ON ONE'S YEARLY INCOME.

NO, I DON'T BELIEVE YOUR FATHER MEANT FOR YOU TO GIVE THEM MONEY. THE ASSISTANCE HE THOUGHT OF WAS ONLY SUCH AS MIGHT REASONABLY BE EXPECTED OF YOU.

HELPING THEM TO FIND A SMALL HOUSE...

HELPING THEM TO MOVE THEIR THINGS...

SENDING THEM PRESENTS OF FISH OR GAME.

AND LEST YOU FORGET, THEY WILL HAVE *FIVE HUNDRED* A YEAR AMONGST THEM. WHAT ON EARTH CAN *FOUR WOMEN* WANT FOR MORE THAN *THAT?*

THEIR HOUSEKEEPING EXPENSES WILL AMOUNT TO NOTHING AT ALL, THEY WILL KEEP LITTLE COMPANY, HAVE FEW SERVANTS, AND NO HORSES OR CARRIAGES.

ONLY CONCEIVE HOW COMFORTABLE THEY WILL BE ON FIVE HUNDRED A YEAR. I CANNOT IMAGINE HOW THEY WILL SPEND HALF OF IT.

AS FOR YOU GIVING THEM MORE, IT IS QUITE ABSURD TO THINK OF IT. THEY WILL BE MUCH MORE ABLE TO GIVE *YOU* SOMETHING.

UPON MY WORD, I BELIEVE YOU ARE RIGHT.

MY FATHER'S REQUEST WAS, JUST AS YOU SAY, THAT I SHOULD FULFILL MY RESPONSIBILITIES WITH ACTS OF ASSISTANCE AND KINDNESS.

WHEN MY MOTHER REMOVES TO ANOTHER HOUSE, MY SERVICES SHALL BE READILY GIVEN TO ACCOMMODATE HER. SOME LITTLE PRESENT OF FURNITURE MIGHT THEN BE ACCEPTABLE.

YET CONSIDER THAT WHEN YOUR FATHER AND HIS WIFE MOVED TO NORLAND, THEY BROUGHT ALL THEIR CHINA, PLATE, AND LINENS WITH THEM.

THIS IS NOW LEFT TO YOUR STEPMOTHER. HER HOUSE WILL BE COMPLETELY FITTED AS SHE TAKES IT.

SOME OF THAT PLATE WOULD HAVE BEEN A VERY NICE ADDITION TO OUR STOCK HERE.

AND THE BREAKFAST CHINA IS TWICE AS HANDSOME AS WHAT BELONGS TO THIS HOUSE. A DEAL TOO HANDSOME FOR ANY PLACE *THEY* CAN AFFORD TO LIVE IN.

BUT SO IT IS...YOUR FATHER THOUGHT ONLY OF THEM...

AND I MUST SAY THIS: YOU OWE NO PARTICULAR GRATITUDE TO HIM, NOR ATTENTION TO HIS WISHES.

WE BOTH KNOW VERY WELL THAT IF HE'D HAD A CHOICE, HE WOULD HAVE LEFT ALMOST EVERYTHING TO THEM.

I FEAR YOU ARE RIGHT.

*T*WO MONTHS AFTER FANNY DASHWOOD HAD ESTABLISHED HERSELF AT NORLAND, HER BROTHER EDWARD FERRARS CAME TO VISIT.

HAVING SUFFERED DAILY COMMERCE WITH THE SISTER, THE DASHWOOD GIRLS WERE PREPARED TO DISLIKE THE BROTHER...

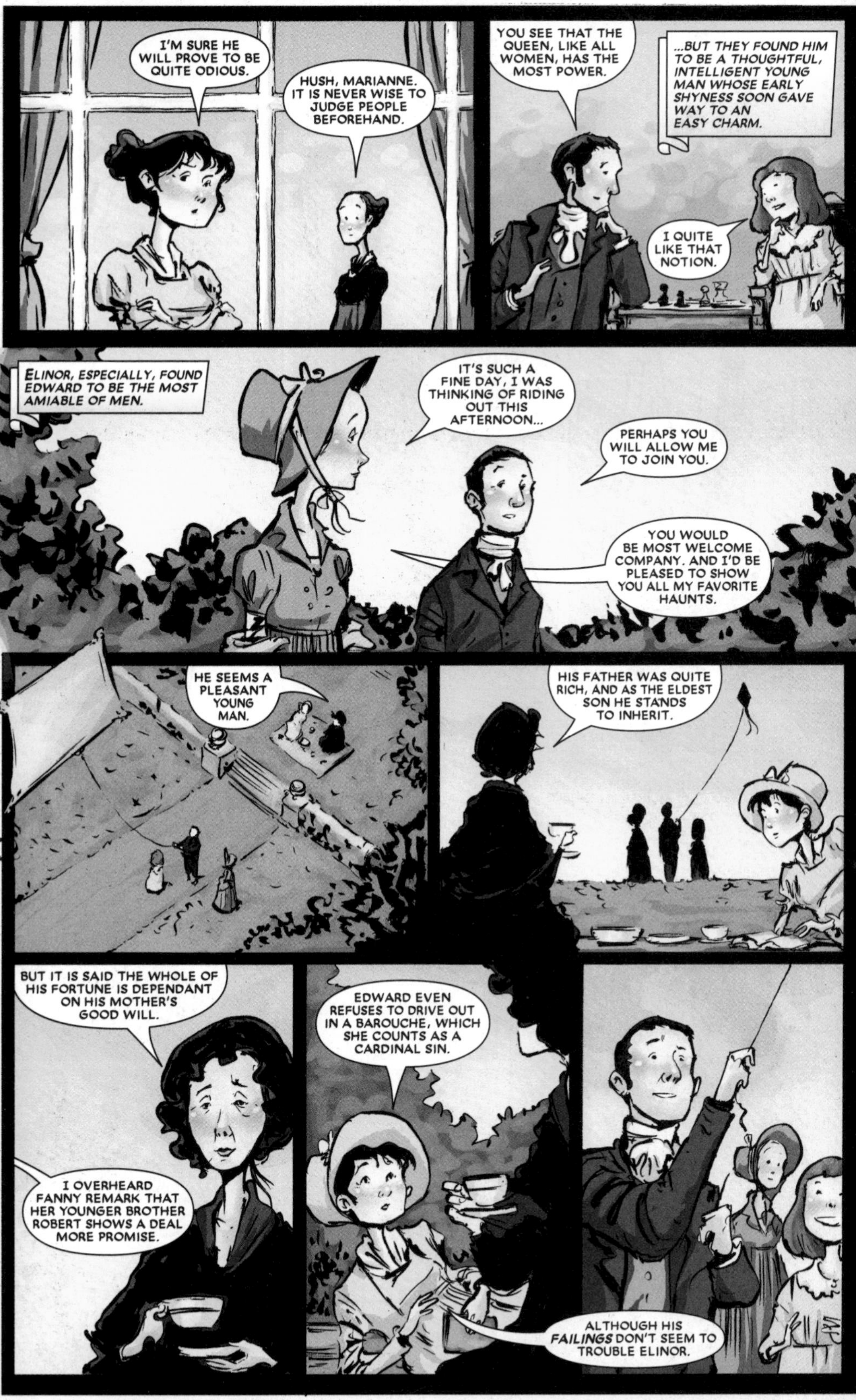
I'M SURE HE WILL PROVE TO BE QUITE ODIOUS.
HUSH, MARIANNE. IT IS NEVER WISE TO JUDGE PEOPLE BEFOREHAND.
YOU SEE THAT THE QUEEN, LIKE ALL WOMEN, HAS THE MOST POWER.
...BUT THEY FOUND HIM TO BE A THOUGHTFUL, INTELLIGENT YOUNG MAN WHOSE EARLY SHYNESS SOON GAVE WAY TO AN EASY CHARM.
I QUITE LIKE THAT NOTION.
ELINOR, ESPECIALLY, FOUND EDWARD TO BE THE MOST AMIABLE OF MEN.
IT'S SUCH A FINE DAY, I WAS THINKING OF RIDING OUT THIS AFTERNOON...
PERHAPS YOU WILL ALLOW ME TO JOIN YOU.
YOU WOULD BE MOST WELCOME COMPANY. AND I'D BE PLEASED TO SHOW YOU ALL MY FAVORITE HAUNTS.
HE SEEMS A PLEASANT YOUNG MAN.
HIS FATHER WAS QUITE RICH, AND AS THE ELDEST SON HE STANDS TO INHERIT.
BUT IT IS SAID THE WHOLE OF HIS FORTUNE IS DEPENDANT ON HIS MOTHER'S GOOD WILL.
I OVERHEARD FANNY REMARK THAT HER YOUNGER BROTHER ROBERT SHOWS A DEAL MORE PROMISE.
EDWARD EVEN REFUSES TO DRIVE OUT IN A BAROUCHE, WHICH SHE COUNTS AS A CARDINAL SIN.
ALTHOUGH HIS *FAILINGS* DON'T SEEM TO TROUBLE ELINOR.

LATER THAT EVENING...

IT DID MY HEART GOOD TO SEE YOU SO HAPPY THIS AFTERNOON, DEAREST.

MR. FERRARS CAN ALWAYS COAX A SMILE FROM ME. UNLIKE HIS SISTER.

TO SAY HE IS UNLIKE FANNY IS ENOUGH. IT IMPLIES EVERYTHING AMIABLE. I LOVE HIM ALREADY.

I THINK YOU WILL LIKE HIM ONCE YOU GET TO KNOW HIM BETTER.

LIKE HIM! I FEEL NO SENTIMENT OF APPROVAL INFERIOR TO LOVE.

YOU MAY ESTEEM HIM, AS I DO.

I HAVE NEVER YET KNOWN WHAT IT IS TO SEPARATE ESTEEM FROM LOVE.

MRS. DASHWOOD NOW TOOK PAINS TO BECOME BETTER ACQUAINTED WITH EDWARD.

IT IS QUITE A NOVELTY TO HAVE A YOUNG MAN ATTEND ME. I COULD GROW TO LIKE IT.

THEN CONSIDER ME AT YOUR SERVICE, MA'AM.

AFTER HIS FIRST VISIT TO NORLAND, EDWARD BEGAN TO SPEND THE GREATEST PART OF HIS TIME THERE.

WE DID NOT EXPECT TO SEE YOU AGAIN SO SOON. IT WAS A PLEASANT SURPRISE.

ALTHOUGH I FANCY YOUR MOTHER MISSES YOU WHEN YOU ARE AWAY FROM LONDON.

SHE HAS MY BROTHER ROBERT TO KEEP HER COMPANY. SHE DOTES ON HIM.

AH, BUT NOT ON YOU?

MY MOTHER AND SISTER LONG TO SEE ME DISTINGUISHED, THOUGH THEY HARDLY KNOW AS WHAT.

MY MOTHER HAD HOPES THAT I MIGHT GO INTO POLITICS OR ATTACH MYSELF TO SOME GREAT MAN.

ALAS, I FEAR I WAS NOT CUT OUT TO BECOME A FINE FIGURE IN THE WORLD.

I SUPPOSE I COULD SAY THE SAME.

I ADMIT IT'S ALL I'VE EVER KNOWN, AND YET IT SUITS ME.

YES, I'D SAY IT SUITS YOU VERY WELL.

THEN YOU ARE NOT AMBITIOUS?

MY ONLY AMBITION IS FOR DOMESTIC COMFORT AND A QUIET LIFE.

IN A FEW MONTHS, MY DEAR, ELINOR WILL IN ALL PROBABILITY BE SETTLED FOR LIFE.

WE SHALL MISS HER, BUT *SHE* WILL BE HAPPY.

BUT, MAMA, HOW SHALL WE GO ON WITHOUT HER?

BE AT EASE, MARIANNE.

I'M SURE MR. FERRARS WILL SEE TO IT THAT WE LIVE WITHIN A FEW MILES OF EACH OTHER AND SHALL MEET EVERY DAY OF OUR LIVES.

YOU WILL GAIN A BROTHER. A *REAL, AFFECTIONATE* BROTHER. I HAVE THE HIGHEST OPINION OF EDWARD'S HEART.

OH, EDWARD IS MOST AMIABLE AND I DO LOVE HIM TENDERLY. BUT YET...

HE IS NOT THE KIND OF YOUNG MAN--

THERE IS SOMETHING WANTING. HIS FIGURE IS NOT STRIKING AND IT HAS NONE OF THAT GRACE I SHOULD EXPECT IN A MAN WHO COULD ATTACH ELINOR.

HIS EYES WANT THE SPIRIT, THE FIRE, THAT ANNOUNCES VIRTUE AND INTELLIGENCE.

AND I AM AFRAID, MAMA, THAT HE HAS NO REAL TASTE. MUSIC SCARCELY ATTRACTS HIM, AND WHILE IT'S TRUE HE ADMIRES ELINOR'S DRAWINGS, IT IS EVIDENT HE KNOWS NOTHING OF ART.

HE ADMIRES AS A LOVER, NOT AS A CONNOISSEUR.

I BELIEVE YOU ARE BEING A BIT HARSH--

TO SATISFY *ME*, THOSE CHARACTERS MUST BE UNITED. I COULD NOT BE HAPPY WITH A MAN WHOSE TASTE DID NOT COINCIDE WITH MY OWN IN EVERY POINT.

HE...HE MUST ENTER INTO ALL MY FEELINGS, THE SAME BOOKS, THE SAME PAINTINGS, THE SAME MUSIC MUST CHARM US.

OH, MAMA, HOW SPIRITLESS AND TAME WAS EDWARD'S READING OF *THE CORSAIR* TO US LAST NIGHT! I FELT FOR ELINOR MOST SEVERELY. YET SHE BORE IT WITH SO MUCH COMPOSURE. I VOW SHE SCARCELY NOTICED IT.

TO HEAR THOSE BEAUTIFUL LINES--WHICH HAVE FREQUENTLY ALMOST DRIVEN ME WILD--PRONOUNCED WITH SUCH DREADFUL INDIFFERENCE!

NO, MAMA, IF HE IS NOT TO BE ANIMATED BY BYRON--!

YOU MUST ALLOW FOR DIFFERENCE OF TASTE, MARIANNE.

IT'S TRUE. ELINOR HAS NOT MY FEELINGS, AND THEREFORE SHE MAY OVERLOOK IT AND BE HAPPY WITH HIM.

BUT IT WOULD HAVE BROKEN MY HEART, HAD I LOVED HIM, TO HEAR HIM READ WITH SUCH LITTLE SENSIBILITY.

THE MORE I KNOW OF THE WORLD, THE MORE I AM CONVINCED THAT I SHALL NEVER MEET A MAN WHOM I CAN REALLY LOVE. I REQUIRE SO MUCH!

HE MUST HAVE ALL EDWARD'S VIRTUES, AND BEYOND THAT HIS PERSON AND MANNERS MUST ORNAMENT HIS GOODNESS WITH EVERY POSSIBLE CHARM.

YOU ARE NOT YET TURNED SEVENTEEN, MY LOVE. TOO EARLY IN LIFE TO DESPAIR OF SUCH HAPPINESS. WHY SHOULD YOU BE LESS FORTUNATE THAN YOUR OWN MOTHER?

IN ONE CIRCUMSTANCE ONLY, DEAR MARIANNE, MAY YOUR DESTINY MAY BE DIFFERENT FROM MINE.

BUT MARIANNE WAS STILL TROUBLED BY ELINOR'S BLINDNESS TOWARD EDWARD'S FLAWS.

WHAT A PITY THAT EDWARD SHOULD HAVE NO TASTE FOR DRAWING.

NO TASTE FOR IT? WHY SHOULD YOU THINK SO?

IT'S TRUE HE DOES NOT DRAW HIMSELF, BUT HE TAKES GREAT PLEASURE IN THE SKILL OF OTHERS.

HAD HE EVER HAD A CHANCE TO LEARN, I THINK HE WOULD HAVE DRAWN VERY WELL.

BUT HE DISTRUSTS HIS OWN JUDGMENT IN SUCH MATTERS, AND SO IS UNWILLING TO GIVE HIS OPINION. YET HE HAS AN INNATE PROPRIETY AND SIMPLICITY OF TASTE, WHICH DIRECT HIM PERFECTLY RIGHT.

I WAS MERELY POINTING OUT THAT HE IS VERY FAR FROM FEELING THE RAPTUROUS DELIGHT IN DRAWINGS AND PAINTING, WHICH, IN MY OPINION, CAN ALONE BE CALLED TASTE.

I HOPE THAT YOU DO NOT CONSIDER HIM DEFICIENT IN TASTE. INDEED, I MUST THINK YOU CANNOT, FOR YOUR BEHAVIOR TO HIM IS PERFECTLY CORDIAL...

...AND IF *THAT* WERE YOUR OPINION, I AM SURE YOU COULD NEVER BE CIVIL TO HIM.

PLEASE DO NOT BE OFFENDED IF MY PRAISE OF HIM IS NOT EQUAL TO YOUR SENSE OF HIS MERITS.

I HAVE NOT HAD AS MANY OPPORTUNITIES OF ESTIMATING HIS INCLINATIONS AND TASTES AS YOU HAVE, BUT BE ASSURED THAT I HAVE THE HIGHEST OPINION OF HIS GOODNESS AND SENSE.

I THINK HIM EVERYTHING THAT IS WORTHY.

I AM SURE THAT EVEN HIS DEAREST FRIENDS COULD NOT BE DISSATISFIED WITH SUCH A COMMENDATION. OF HIS SENSE AND GOODNESS, NO ONE WHO HAS ENGAGED HIM IN UNRESERVED CONVERSATION CAN BE IN DOUBT.

ALAS, THE EXCELLENCE OF HIS UNDERSTANDING AND HIS PRINCIPLES ARE ONLY CONCEALED BY HIS SHYNESS, WHICH TOO OFTEN KEEPS HIM SILENT.

I HAVE SEEN A GREAT DEAL OF HIM, AND I VENTURE TO PRONOUNCE THAT HIS MIND IS WELL-INFORMED AND HIS IMAGINATION LIVELY.

HIS ABILITIES IN EVERY RESPECT IMPROVE AS MUCH UPON ACQUAINTANCE AS HIS MANNERS AND PERSON.

AT FIRST SIGHT, HIS ADDRESS IS NOT STRIKING AND HIS PERSON CAN HARDLY BE CALLED HANDSOME, UNTIL THE EXPRESSION IN HIS EYES, WHICH ARE UNCOMMONLY GOOD, AND THE SWEETNESS OF HIS COUNTENANCE ARE PERCEIVED.

AT PRESENT, I KNOW HIM SO WELL THAT I THINK HIM QUITE HANDSOME, OR AT LEAST, ALMOST SO.

WHAT SAY YOU, MARIANNE?

I SHALL VERY SOON THINK HIM HANDSOME IF I DO NOT NOW...

...WHEN YOU TELL ME TO LOVE HIM AS A BROTHER.

I--I FEEL I'VE BEEN BETRAYED INTO SAYING TOO MUCH.

I UNDERSTAND THAT WITH YOU-- AND WITH MAMA-- WISHING LEADS TO HOPING AND HOPING TO EXPECTATIONS.

BUT AS TO ANY MUTUAL REGARD OR UNDERSTANDING BETWEEN EDWARD AND MYSELF, I REQUIRE GREATER CERTAINTY TO SPEAK OF IT WITH ANY COMFORT.

WHAT OF *YOUR* REGARD?

I WON'T ATTEMPT TO DENY THAT I THINK VERY HIGHLY OF HIM. THAT I...ESTEEM AND LIKE HIM.

ESTEEM HIM! *LIKE* HIM!

COLD-HEARTED ELINOR! OH, WORSE THAN COLD-HEARTED, FOR YOU ARE ASHAMED OF BEING OTHERWISE. IF YOU USE THOSE WORDS AGAIN, I SHALL LEAVE THE ROOM.

DO EXCUSE ME, MY DEAREST HOTHEAD.

AND BE ASSURED THAT I MEANT NO OFFENSE TO YOU BY SPEAKING, IN SO QUIET A WAY, OF MY OWN FEELINGS. I GIVE YOU LEAVE TO BELIEVE THEM TO BE STRONGER THAN I HAVE DECLARED.

BELIEVE THEM TO BE SUCH AS HIS MERIT--AND THE HOPE OF HIS AFFECTION FOR ME--MAY WARRANT. BUT FARTHER THAN THAT YOU MUST NOT BELIEVE.

I AM BY NO MEANS ASSURED OF HIS REGARD FOR ME.

UNTIL HIS SENTIMENTS ARE KNOWN, YOU CANNOT BLAME ME FOR WISHING TO AVOID ANY ENCOURAGEMENT OF MY PARTIALITY BY BELIEVING OR CALLING IT MORE THAN IT IS.

AND ALTHOUGH, IN MY HEART, I FEEL SCARCELY ANY DOUBT OF HIS PREFERENCE, THERE ARE OTHER POINTS TO CONSIDER.

HE IS VERY FAR FROM INDEPENDENT, AND FROM FANNY'S COMMENTS ABOUT THEIR MOTHER, WE HAVE LITTLE REASON TO THINK HER AMIABLE.

AND I AM SURE EDWARD IS QUITE AWARE OF THE DIFFICULTIES HE WOULD FACE IF HE WERE TO MARRY A WOMAN WITH NEITHER A FORTUNE NOR HIGH RANK.

SO YOU REALLY ARE NOT ENGAGED TO HIM. MAMA SEEMED TO THINK IT A *FAIT ACCOMPLI*. YET IT CERTAINLY WILL HAPPEN SOON.

IN THE MEANTIME I SEE TWO ADVANTAGES TO THE DELAY--I WILL NOT LOSE YOU SO QUICKLY, AND EDWARD WILL HAVE THE OPPORTUNITY OF IMPROVING THAT NATURAL TASTE WHICH WILL BE SO NECESSARY TO YOUR FUTURE HAPPINESS.

OH, IF HE SHOULD BE INSPIRED BY YOU TO LEARN TO DRAW HIMSELF, HOW DELIGHTFUL IT WOULD BE!

I WISH I COULD BE AS ASSURED OF THE OUTCOME. THINGS ARE NOT IN SO PROSPEROUS A STATE AS MY SISTER WOULD LIKE TO BELIEVE.

I CANNOT DENY THERE IS, AT TIMES, A LACK OF SPIRIT ABOUT EDWARD. NOT INDIFFERENCE, PRECISELY, BUT IT MAKES ME DOUBTFUL OF THE NATURE OF HIS REGARD.

PERHAPS I SHOULD ACCUSTOM MYSELF TO THE NOTION THAT IT IS NOTHING MORE THAN FRIENDSHIP HE FEELS.

IT WAS ONLY A MATTER OF TIME BEFORE FANNY...

WHO RARELY LOOKED BEYOND HER OWN CONCERNS...

YE BOOK STORE

GREW AWARE OF EDWARD'S PARTIALITY FOR ELINOR.

SHE TOOK THE FIRST OPPORTUNITY TO CONFRONT MRS. DASHWOOD ON THE MATTER.

I ASKED TO SPEAK WITH YOU ON A MOST...*URGENT* MATTER. AS YOU KNOW, DURING THE PAST SIX MONTHS MY BROTHER HAS BEEN A FREQUENT VISITOR HERE.

A MOST WELCOME VISITOR, I COULD ADD. MR. FERRARS HAS BECOME A FAVORITE WITH ALL MY DAUGHTERS. I MYSELF FIND HIS COMPANY DELIGHTFUL.

AND I *ASSUME* YOU ARE AWARE OF THE GREAT PLANS MY MOTHER HAS FOR EDWARD, NAY, FOR BOTH MY BROTHERS.

IT IS HER FONDEST WISH THAT THEY RISE TO THE HIGHEST LEVELS OF GOVERNMENT, AN EXPECTATION THAT IS WELL WITHIN THEIR MEANS OF ACHIEVING, CONSIDERING THE FUNDS AT HER DISPOSAL AND HER MANY CONNECTIONS IN LONDON.

I DOUBT THERE IS LITTLE MR. FERRARS COULD NOT ACHIEVE, WERE HIS HEART SET ON IT.

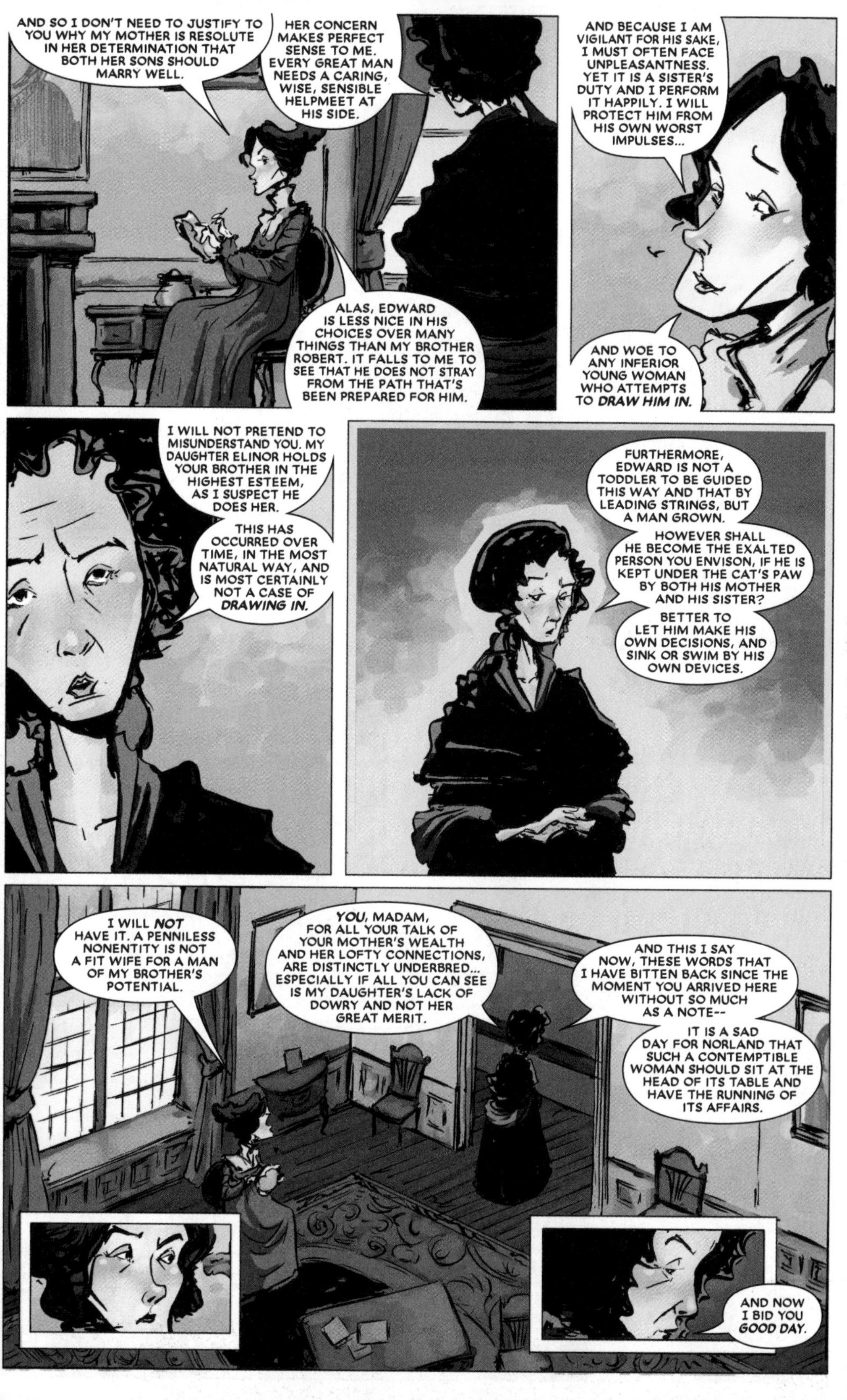
AND SO I DON'T NEED TO JUSTIFY TO YOU WHY MY MOTHER IS RESOLUTE IN HER DETERMINATION THAT BOTH HER SONS SHOULD MARRY WELL.
HER CONCERN MAKES PERFECT SENSE TO ME. EVERY GREAT MAN NEEDS A CARING, WISE, SENSIBLE HELPMEET AT HIS SIDE.
ALAS, EDWARD IS LESS NICE IN HIS CHOICES OVER MANY THINGS THAN MY BROTHER ROBERT. IT FALLS TO ME TO SEE THAT HE DOES NOT STRAY FROM THE PATH THAT'S BEEN PREPARED FOR HIM.
AND BECAUSE I AM VIGILANT FOR HIS SAKE, I MUST OFTEN FACE UNPLEASANTNESS. YET IT IS A SISTER'S DUTY AND I PERFORM IT HAPPILY. I WILL PROTECT HIM FROM HIS OWN WORST IMPULSES...
AND WOE TO ANY INFERIOR YOUNG WOMAN WHO ATTEMPTS TO *DRAW HIM IN.*
I WILL NOT PRETEND TO MISUNDERSTAND YOU. MY DAUGHTER ELINOR HOLDS YOUR BROTHER IN THE HIGHEST ESTEEM, AS I SUSPECT HE DOES HER.
THIS HAS OCCURRED OVER TIME, IN THE MOST NATURAL WAY, AND IS MOST CERTAINLY NOT A CASE OF *DRAWING IN.*
FURTHERMORE, EDWARD IS NOT A TODDLER TO BE GUIDED THIS WAY AND THAT BY LEADING STRINGS, BUT A MAN GROWN.
HOWEVER SHALL HE BECOME THE EXALTED PERSON YOU ENVISON, IF HE IS KEPT UNDER THE CAT'S PAW BY BOTH HIS MOTHER AND HIS SISTER?
BETTER TO LET HIM MAKE HIS OWN DECISIONS, AND SINK OR SWIM BY HIS OWN DEVICES.
I WILL *NOT* HAVE IT. A PENNILESS NONENTITY IS NOT A FIT WIFE FOR A MAN OF MY BROTHER'S POTENTIAL.
YOU, MADAM, FOR ALL YOUR TALK OF YOUR MOTHER'S WEALTH AND HER LOFTY CONNECTIONS, ARE DISTINCTLY UNDERBRED... ESPECIALLY IF ALL YOU CAN SEE IS MY DAUGHTER'S LACK OF DOWRY AND NOT HER GREAT MERIT.
AND THIS I SAY NOW, THESE WORDS THAT I HAVE BITTEN BACK SINCE THE MOMENT YOU ARRIVED HERE WITHOUT SO MUCH AS A NOTE--
IT IS A SAD DAY FOR NORLAND THAT SUCH A CONTEMPTIBLE WOMAN SHOULD SIT AT THE HEAD OF ITS TABLE AND HAVE THE RUNNING OF ITS AFFAIRS.
AND NOW I BID YOU *GOOD DAY.*

WE MUST LEAVE THIS PLACE AT ONCE. I WON'T HAVE ELINOR EXPOSED TO THAT WOMAN'S INSINUATIONS.

BY A HAPPY COINCIDENCE, MRS. DASHWOOD'S PROBLEMS WERE RESOLVED IN THE NEXT DAY'S POST.

IT IS FROM MY DISTANT RELATION, SIR JOHN MIDDLETON OF BARTON PARK.

HE WRITES THAT HE HAS A SMALL HOUSE TO LET ON VERY EASY TERMS, AND THAT HE WILL DO EVERYTHING WE REQUIRE TO MAKE IT COMFORTABLE.

WHERE IS BARTON PARK, MAMA?

BUT THAT'S SO FAR FROM SUSSEX, FROM ALL THAT IS FAMILIAR TO US. I DARESAY WE SHALL NEVER SEE OUR FRIENDS AGAIN.

YES, IT WILL BE QUITE A CHANGE. BUT NOW THAT I THINK ON IT, IT MIGHT BE PRUDENT TO SETTLE SOME DISTANCE FROM HERE. ELSE WE WILL ALWAYS BE REMINDED OF OUR FORMER LIVES IN NORLAND.

IN DEVON WE WILL TRULY BE MAKING A FRESH START.

IT'S IN DEVONSHIRE, PET. JUST NORTH OF EXETER.

THERE, THAT'S MY WISE ELINOR. A FRESH START, INDEED.

THE NEXT DAY, MRS. DASHWOOD HAD THE PLEASURE OF ANNOUNCING TO HER STEPSON AND HIS WIFE THAT SHE HAD BEEN PROVIDED WITH A HOUSE.

I HOPE YOU'RE NOT REMOVING TOO FAR FROM NORLAND.

WE'RE GOING TO MY COUSIN, SIR JOHN MIDDLETON, IN DEVONSHIRE. HE'S OFFERED US A SMALL HOUSE ON HIS PROPERTY.

DEVONSHIRE!

ARE YOU, INDEED, MOVING TO A PLACE YOU'VE NEVER SEEN?

YES, AND WITHIN THE WEEK. IT IS BUT A COTTAGE, BUT I HOPE TO SEE ALL MY FRIENDS THERE.

IF THEY FIND NO DIFFICULTY IN TRAVELING SO FAR TO VISIT ME, I WILL FIND NONE IN ACCOMMODATING THEM.

JOHN, YOU AND FANNY ARE ALSO INCLUDED IN MY INVITATION.

AND EDWARD, MY DEAR BOY, WE WOULD ESPECIALLY WELCOME YOU.

I AM SORRY DEVON IS SUCH A DISTANCE AWAY...

I WOULD HAVE LIKED TO HAVE BEEN OF SERVICE TO YOU IN THE REMOVAL OF YOUR FURNITURE TO A NEARBY DWELLING. BUT ALAS, NOW...

OUR THINGS WILL BE SENT AROUND BY WATER. THE HOUSE IS NOT FAR FROM THE COAST.

ALTHOUGH I DON'T MEAN TO TURN DOWN ANY OFFERS OF *ASSISTANCE*.

WELL THEN, I PROMISE TO SEND YOU A BASKET OF GAME ONCE THE COVERTS ARE STOCKED.

AND PERHAPS SOME SALTED FISH OVER THE HOLIDAY SEASON.

YES, I ALWAYS EXPECTED YOU WOULD...LOOK AFTER US.

IN YOUR WAY.

LATER THAT SAME DAY...

I'VE BEEN LOOKING OVER OUR FINANCES, MAMA, AND IT IS NOT VERY HEARTENING.

I GATHER THAT JOHN HAS NOT SETTLED ANY MONEY ON YOU, IN SPITE OF HIS PROMISE TO PAPA.

YOU DEAR FATHER HAS BEEN GONE THESE SIX MONTHS AND NOT ONE WORD HAVE I HAD FROM YOUR BROTHER ON THE MATTER.

I DID NOT THINK HIM SO LOST TO HIS OBLIGATIONS THAT HE WOULD ABANDON US IN SUCH A WAY.

YOU HEARD HIM THIS MORNING. HE INTENDS TO SEND US *FISH*.

THEN WE SHALL BE HARD PRESSED TO MAKE DUE AND MUST PRACTICE ECONOMY AT EVERY TURN.

DON'T FRET, DEAREST. HOW DIFFICULT CAN IT BE TO KEEP OUR EXPENSES DOWN?

WE SHALL LIVE A SIMPLE COUNTRY LIFE WITH ALL ITS INHERENT PLEASURES.

A FEW DAYS BEFORE THE LADIES WERE TO DEPART, FANNY TOOK STOCK.

THIS IS MUCH TOO FINE FOR A COUNTRY COTTAGE.

ACH, THESE ARE MUCH FINER THAN ANYTHING JOHN OR I POSSESS. THEY WOULD DO CREDIT TO OUR TOWNHOUSE IN LONDON.

IT'S QUITE IMPOSSIBLE TO COMPREHEND WHY, WITH SUCH A TRIFLING INCOME, THESE DASHWOODS SHOULD HAVE ANY HANDSOME PIECES OF FURNITURE AT ALL.

FINALLY...

THE FATEFUL DAY ARRIVED.

MANY WERE THE TEARS SHED BY THE DASHWOODS IN THEIR LAST ADIEUS TO A PLACE SO MUCH BELOVED.

GOODBYE, DEAR, DEAR NORLAND.

WHEN SHALL I CEASE TO REGRET YOU!-- WHEN LEARN TO FEEL A HOME ELSEWHERE!--OH! HAPPY HOUSE, COULD YOU KNOW WHAT I SUFFER IN NOW VIEWING YOU FROM THIS SPOT, FROM WHENCE PERHAPS I MAY VIEW YOU NO MORE?

NO. YOU WILL CONTINUE THE SAME, UNCONSCIOUS OF THE PLEASURE OR THE REGRET YOU OCCASION! BUT WHO WILL REMAIN TO ENJOY YOU?

YOUR SISTER, AS ALWAYS, WEARS HER HEART ON HER SLEEVE.

IT'S TRUE THAT MARIANNE CAN APPEAR TO HAVE AN EXCESS OF SENSIBILITY AT TIMES, BUT THIS MORNING SHE IS ONLY SAYING WHAT IS IN MY HEART, AS WELL.

IT MUST BE DIFFICULT TO LEAVE YOUR HOME OF SO MANY YEARS.

IT IS. QUITE DIFFICULT.

BUT WE ARE FORTUNATE THAT WE WILL STILL BE ALL TOGETHER IN THE NEW HOUSE.

YOU...YOU MUST COME AND VISIT.

OF COURSE I WILL. I DON'T DARE DISAPPOINT CAPTAIN MARGARET. SHE'LL HAVE ME ON THE YARDARM.

I WISH YOU A SAFE JOURNEY, MISS DASHWOOD, AND A MOST HAPPY ARRIVAL.

THANK YOU, EDW--MR. FERRARS.

COME, GIRLS, THE TIME FOR LAMENTATIONS IS DONE. IT'S BEST IF WE WERE OFF NOW.

BUT WHERE ARE JOHN AND FANNY? IS NO ONE BUT EDWARD TO SEE US OFF?

YOUR BROTHER WAS CALLED TO THE HOME FARM THIS MORNING.

AND FANNY, WELL...

I SUPPOSE SHE HAS OTHER THINGS TO OCCUPY HER.

LET US BE HOPEFUL. PERHAPS OUR WELCOME IN DEVON WILL PROVE MORE LIVELY THAN OUR FAREWELL IN SUSSEX.

GOOD-BYYYE, EDWWWARD!

I SHOULDN'T DOUBT IT. SIR JOHN IS THE MOST GOODHEARTED OF MEN. QUITE A SPORTSMAN, AS WELL.

IT'S LIKELY HE HAS A HOUSEFUL OF GUESTS DOWN FOR THE SHOOTING AND HUNTING. I EXPECT YOU AND MARIANNE WON'T LACK FOR COMPANY.

*A*FTER SUFFERING SEVERAL DAYS OF WEARYING TRAVEL AND MELANCHOLY DISPOSITIONS, THE DASHWOOD LADIES REACHED THE SWEEPING GREEN MOORS OF SOUTH DEVON.

THERE IT IS! THAT MUST BE BARTON PARK.

WHAT A PLEASANT AND FERTILE SPOT, SO WELL WOODED AND RICH IN PASTURE.

AND *THAT* MUST BE BARTON COTTAGE.

OH, MAMA, IT IS SO SMALL AND...GRAY.

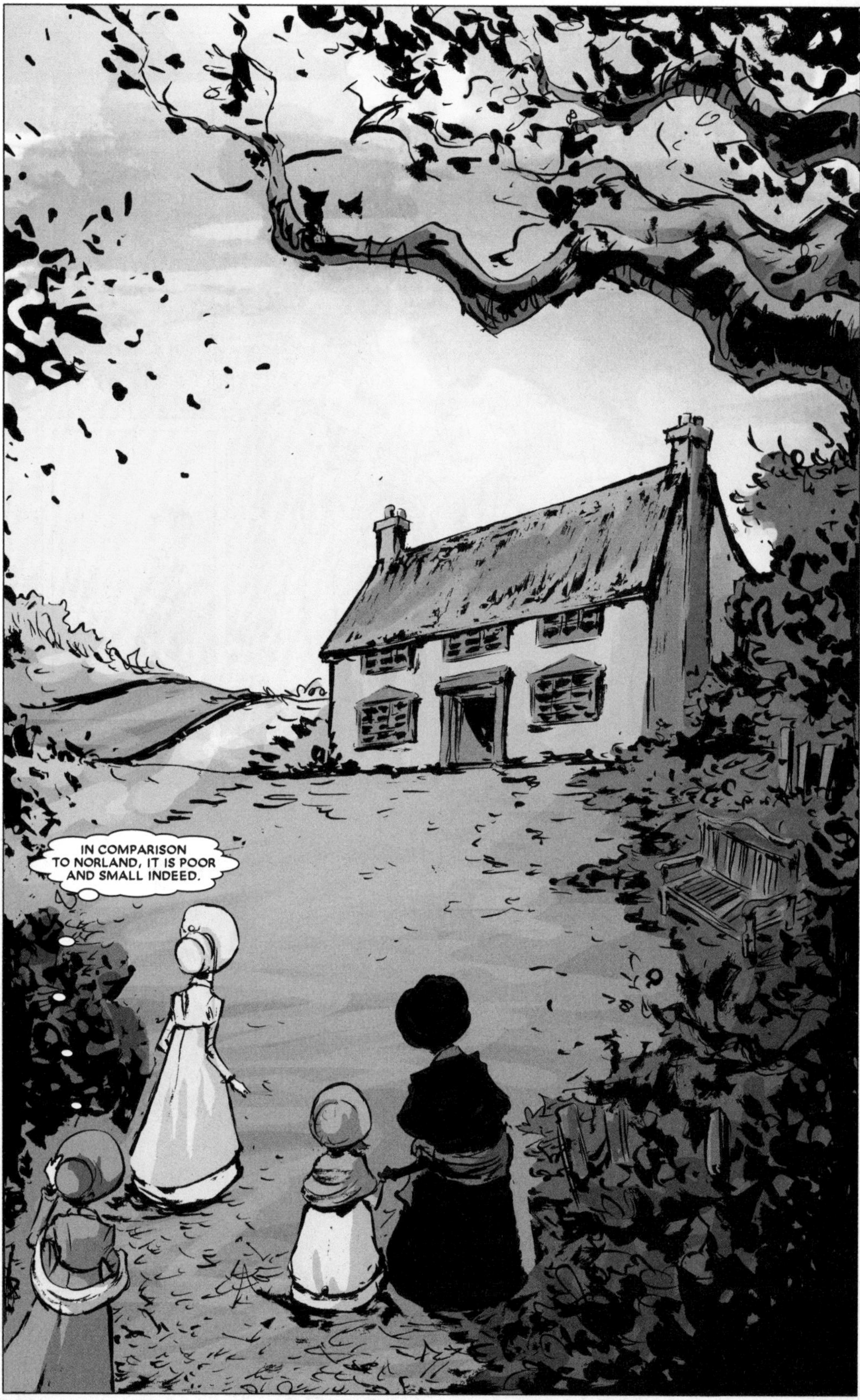
IN COMPARISON TO NORLAND, IT IS POOR AND SMALL INDEED.

THE EVENING OF THEIR ARRIVAL, THE DASHWOOD LADIES TOOK STOCK OF THEIR NEW HOME.

TO BE SURE, THE HOUSE IS TOO SMALL FOR OUR FAMILY.

AND THE PARLORS ARE NOT ADEQUATE FOR THE PARTIES OF OUR FRIENDS I HOPE TO SEE COLLECTED HERE.

PERHAPS IN THE SPRING, IF I HAVE PLENTY OF MONEY, WE MAY THINK ABOUT BUILDING.

ALAS, SHE HAS SUCH HIGH HOPES FOR A WOMAN WHO HAS NEVER SAVED A GROAT IN HER LIFE.

ONCE WE HAVE PLACED OUR BOOKS AND OTHER POSSESSIONS AROUND THE ROOMS, I DARESAY IT WILL BE QUITE COMFORTABLE.

SO THE DASHWOODS SET ABOUT MAKING THE HUMBLE COTTAGE A TRUE HOME.

SEVERAL DAYS LATER, THEIR BREAKFAST WAS INTERRUPTED BY A VISIT FROM THEIR LANDLORD.

WELL MET, DEAREST COUSIN! WELCOME TO BARTON PARK.

YOU MUST TELL ME IF YOU REQUIRE ANYTHING, FRUIT OR GAME AND SUCH. I PRESS YOU TO DINE WITH US TONIGHT AND EVERY NIGHT UNTIL YOU HAVE SETTLED IN.

NAY, I INSIST ON IT.

SIR JOHN, AT LAST I CAN THANK YOU IN PERSON FOR YOUR GENEROSITY.

THAT IS MOST KIND, COUSIN.

ALLOW ME TO MAKE YOU KNOWN TO MY DAUGHTERS, ELINOR, MARIANNE AND MARGARET.

...WE HAVE ANOTHER GUEST WITH US, AS WELL...MY FRIEND, COLONEL BRANDON. A MOST ADMIRABLE GENTLEMAN, AND A BACHELOR OF SOME MEANS.

THEN WE LOOK FORWARD TO SEEING YOU THIS EVENING, COUSIN.

I'M PLEASED THE LONG JOURNEY HAS NOT DIMINISHED THE BLOOM OF YOUR DAUGHTERS. SUCH ROSES YOU HAVE BORNE, MA'AM!

WE MUST SEE ABOUT FINDING SUITORS FOR ELINOR AND MARIANNE.

AH, BUT I CAN SAFELY LEAVE THAT TO LADY MIDDLETON'S MAMA. SHE IS ARRIVING TODAY FOR A VISIT AND IS THE VERY SOUL OF LIVELINESS.

AS THE DAY WANED, THE DASHWOODS DULY MADE THEIR WAY TO BARTON PARK.

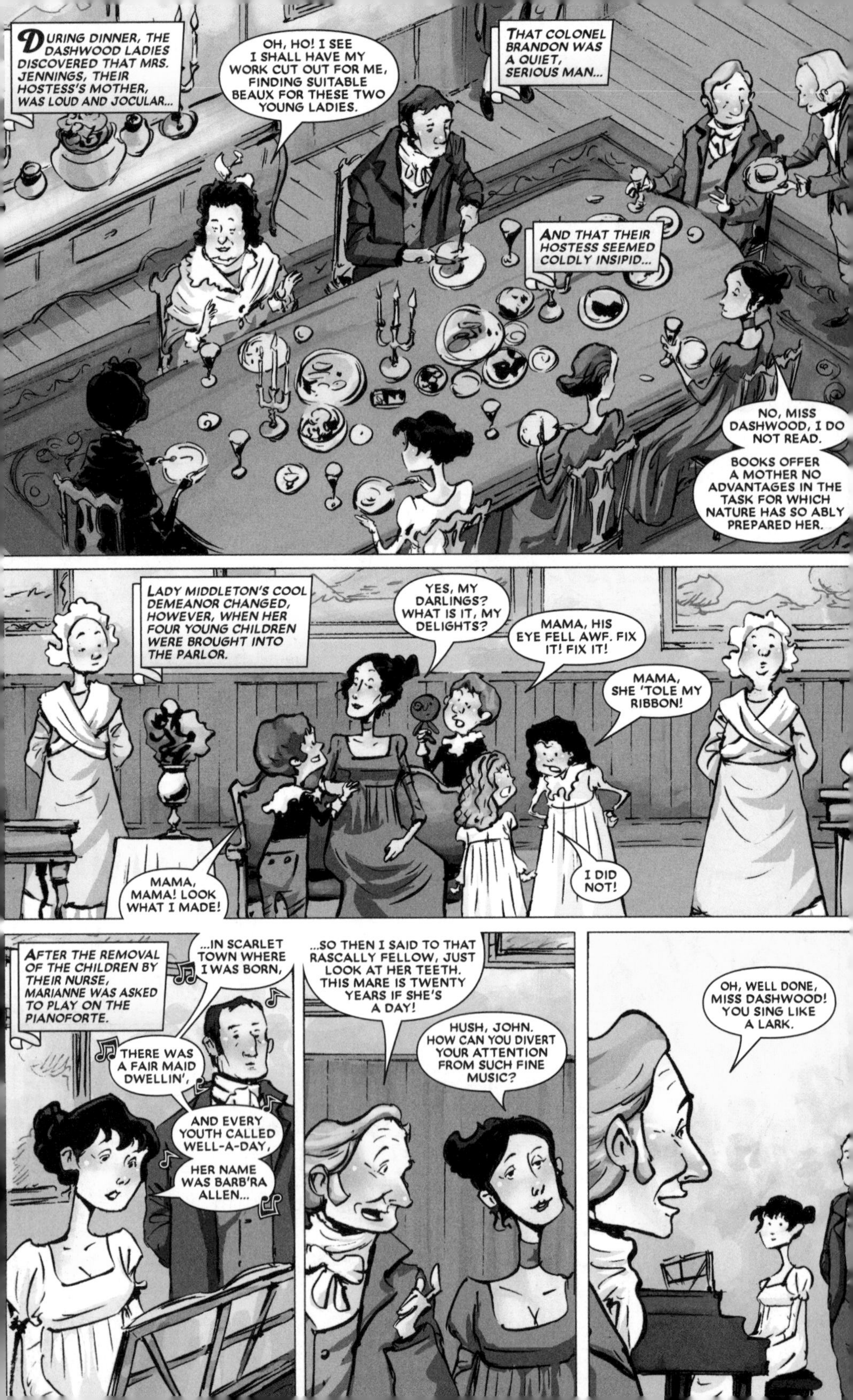
DURING DINNER, THE DASHWOOD LADIES DISCOVERED THAT MRS. JENNINGS, THEIR HOSTESS'S MOTHER, WAS LOUD AND JOCULAR...
OH, HO! I SEE I SHALL HAVE MY WORK CUT OUT FOR ME, FINDING SUITABLE BEAUX FOR THESE TWO YOUNG LADIES.
THAT COLONEL BRANDON WAS A QUIET, SERIOUS MAN...
AND THAT THEIR HOSTESS SEEMED COLDLY INSIPID...
NO, MISS DASHWOOD, I DO NOT READ.
BOOKS OFFER A MOTHER NO ADVANTAGES IN THE TASK FOR WHICH NATURE HAS SO ABLY PREPARED HER.
LADY MIDDLETON'S COOL DEMEANOR CHANGED, HOWEVER, WHEN HER FOUR YOUNG CHILDREN WERE BROUGHT INTO THE PARLOR.
YES, MY DARLINGS? WHAT IS IT, MY DELIGHTS?
MAMA, HIS EYE FELL AWF. FIX IT! FIX IT!
MAMA, SHE 'TOLE MY RIBBON!
MAMA, MAMA! LOOK WHAT I MADE!
I DID NOT!
AFTER THE REMOVAL OF THE CHILDREN BY THEIR NURSE, MARIANNE WAS ASKED TO PLAY ON THE PIANOFORTE.
...IN SCARLET TOWN WHERE I WAS BORN,
THERE WAS A FAIR MAID DWELLIN',
AND EVERY YOUTH CALLED WELL-A-DAY,
HER NAME WAS BARB'RA ALLEN...
...SO THEN I SAID TO THAT RASCALLY FELLOW, JUST LOOK AT HER TEETH. THIS MARE IS TWENTY YEARS IF SHE'S A DAY!
HUSH, JOHN. HOW CAN YOU DIVERT YOUR ATTENTION FROM SUCH FINE MUSIC?
OH, WELL DONE, MISS DASHWOOD! YOU SING LIKE A LARK.

I WAS ONCE QUITE ACCOMPLISHED MYSELF, UNTIL I FORSOOK MUSIC FOR MOTHERHOOD.

I'VE ALWAYS BEEN PARTIAL TO THE BALLAD BARBARA ALLEN, MISS DASHWOOD. I DON'T SUPPOSE YOU KNOW IT.

BUT THAT IS WHAT I JUST--

WHAT SAY WE ASK MISS MARIANNE FOR SOMETHING A BIT MORE LIVELY? PERHAPS A LITTLE MOZART.

I'M SORRY TO SAY NO ONE IN THE PARTY RECOMMENDED THEMSELVES TO ME AS A COMPANION.

LADY MIDDLETON WAS ICY IN THE EXTREME, SAVE WITH HER CHILDREN, AND COLONEL BRANDON IS SERIOUS AS THE GRAVE.

AT LEAST HE PAID ATTENTION WHILE YOU WERE PLAYING. AND YOU MUST ADMIT THAT SIR JOHN AND MRS. JENNINGS PROVIDED SOME MIRTH WITH THEIR BOISTEROUS BEHAVIOR.

BUT THOSE CHILDREN...LADY MIDDLETON LET'S THEM RUN WILD AS LITTLE SAVAGES.

MRS. JENNINGS, THAT TIRELESS GOSSIP, SOON BECAME A FREQUENT VISITOR AT BARTON COTTAGE...AND ONE DAY MADE A SURPRISING ANNOUNCEMENT.

THE INSTANT I MET COLONEL BRANDON, I DETERMINED TO FIND HIM A WIFE, FOR IT IS WELL KNOWN THAT A MAN DOES NOT THRIVE IN THE SINGLE STATE.

AND I'M SURE YOU NOTICED, MISS MARIANNE, HOW HE SITS IN RAPT ATTENTION WHENEVER YOU PLAY FOR US. I AM QUITE CERTAIN HE IS IN LOVE WITH YOU.

NO, DON'T BLUSH. IT WOULD BE AN EXCELLENT MATCH. HE IS RICH AND YOU ARE HANDSOME.

YOU MUST BE MISTAKEN, MA'AM. THE COLONEL WAS MERELY BEING GENTLEMANLY.

YOU CAN DENY IT, PUSS, BUT I KNOW WHAT I SAW. IT MUST BE SO.

LATER THAT DAY, MARIANNE BROACHED HER MOTHER AND SISTER ON MRS. JENNINGS'S STARTLING REVELATION.

I HARDLY KNEW WHETHER TO LAUGH AT THE NOTION, OR TO RAIL AT MRS. JENNINGS FOR HER IMPERTINENCE.

HOW COULD SHE MAKE LIGHT OF THE COLONEL'S ADVANCED YEARS OR MOCK HIS CONDITION AS AN OLD BACHELOR?

OLD?

I DARESAY HE IS NOT ABOVE FIVE AND THIRTY YEARS. HARDLY IN HIS DOTAGE.

HE IS OLD ENOUGH TO BE MY FATHER...AND IF HE WERE EVER ANIMATED ENOUGH TO BE IN LOVE, HE MUST HAVE LONG OUTLIVED EVERY SENSATION OF THE KIND.

IT IS TOO RIDICULOUS. WHEN IS A MAN TO BE SAFE FROM SUCH WIT, IF AGE AND INFIRMITY WILL NOT PROTECT HIM?

INFIRMITY! DO YOU CALL COLONEL BRANDON INFIRM?

HIS AGE MAY APPEAR GREATER TO YOU THAN TO OUR MOTHER, BUT YOU CAN HARDLY DECEIVE YOURSELF AS TO HIS HAVING THE USE OF HIS LIMBS!

AT THIS RATE, YOU MUST BE IN CONTINUAL TERROR OF MY DECAY, AND IT MUST SEEM A MIRACLE TO YOU THAT I HAVE REACHED THE AGE OF FORTY.

DID YOU NOT HEAR HIM COMPLAIN OF HIS RHEUMATISM?

IS THAT NOT THE COMMONEST INFIRMITY OF DECLINING LIFE?

I *KNOW* COLONEL BRANDON IS NOT YET OLD ENOUGH TO MAKE HIS FRIENDS APPREHENSIVE OF LOSING HIM.

BUT HE SPOKE OF FLANNEL WAISTCOATS, WHICH IN MY MIND CONNECTS HIM TO EVERY AILMENT THAT INFLICTS THE OLD AND FEEBLE.

BY THAT RECKONING, THIRTY-FIVE CAN HAVE NOTHING TO DO WITH MATRIMONY.

HAD HE BEEN IN A VIOLENT FEVER, HE MIGHT HAVE RECOMMENDED HIMSELF TO YOU MORE READILY.

CONFESS, MARIANNE, YOU ARE DRAWN TO THE FLUSHED CHEEK, THE HOLLOW EYE, AND THE QUICK PULSE OF A FEVER.

YOU TAKE PLEASURE IN MISUNDERSTANDING ME.

AFTER ELINOR WENT OFF TO HER ROOM...

SPEAKING OF ILLNESS, MAMA, I HAVE A CONCERN THAT I CANNOT CONCEAL FROM YOU.

I FEAR THAT EDWARD FERRARS IS NOT WELL. WE HAVE BEEN HERE A FORTNIGHT, AND YET HE HAS NOT COME.

NOTHING BUT REAL INDISPOSITION COULD CAUSE THIS EXTRAORDINARY DELAY.

WHAT ELSE COULD BE KEEPING HIM AT NORLAND?

DID YOU EXPECT HIM SO SOON? I DID NOT. IF I FEEL ANY ANXIETY, IT IS THAT HE SOMETIMES SHOWED A LACK OF PLEASURE OR READINESS IN ACCEPTING MY INVITATIONS TO VISIT US HERE.

DOES ELINOR EXPECT HIM ALREADY?

I HAVE NEVER MENTIONED IT TO HER...

BUT OF COURSE SHE MUST.

I THINK YOU ARE MISTAKEN.

WHEN I ASKED HER ABOUT GETTING A NEW GRATE FOR THE SPARE BEDCHAMBER, SHE OBSERVED THERE WAS NO HURRY, AS WE WEREN'T LIKELY TO NEED IT FOR SOME TIME.

WHAT CAN BE THE MEANING OF THIS? THE WHOLE OF THEIR BEHAVIOR TO EACH OTHER HAS BEEN UNACCOUNTABLE! HOW COMPOSED WERE THEIR ADIEUS, HOW LANGUID THEIR CONVERSATION THAT LAST EVENING.

IN EDWARD'S FAREWELL, THERE WAS NO DISTINCTION BETWEEN ELINOR AND ME.

AND ELINOR, IN QUITTING NORLAND, NEVER CRIED AS I DID. EVEN NOW HER SELF-COMMAND IS INVARIABLE.

WHEN IS SHE DEJECTED OR MELANCHOLY?

ELINOR HAS ALWAYS KEPT HER OWN COUNSEL. YOU KNOW THAT, MARIANNE.

WITH NO CARRIAGE, MRS. DASHWOOD ONLY VISITED NEIGHBORS WITHIN WALKING DISTANCE.

ALAS, THERE WERE FEW NEIGHBORS WHO COULD BE SO CLASSED.

GOOD DAY TO YOU, VICAR.

ERR, IS THAT YOU, MRS. DASHWOOD? MY EYESIGHT IS NOT WHAT IT WAS.

SO HER GIRLS TOOK TO THE MOORS TO EXPLORE THEIR NEW NEIGHBORHOOD ON FOOT.

HAVE YOU EVER SEEN SUCH A PLACE? IT COULD BE A CASTLE FROM THE DAYS OF KING ARTHUR.

A PITY, THEN, THAT THERE ARE NO GALLANT KNIGHTS JOUSTING IN THE FIELDS.

THAT MUST BE ALLENHAM COURT. ACCORDING TO SIR JOHN, IT IS HOME TO AN INFIRM, ELDERLY LADY.

THEY EVEN UNEARTHED A MYSTERY OF SORTS...

SOON ENOUGH...

THANK GOODNESS! THE RAIN HAS FINALLY STOPPED AFTER TWO DAYS OF DOWNPOUR.

DO EITHER OF YOU FANCY A WALK?

IT'S JUST A BREAK IN THE CLOUDS. THE RAIN IS BOUND TO START UP AGAIN.

I'LL COME WITH YOU, MARIANNE.

IS THERE A FELICITY IN THE WORLD THAT IS SUPERIOR TO THIS?

WE WILL WALK HERE AT LEAST TWO HOURS.

BUT NATURE, ALAS, IS NOT ALWAYS AN ALLY...

A dramatic encounter

RUN!! FASTER, MARIANNE!

LOOK, THERE'S OUR GATE--

O-O-OH!

KRAKKABOOOOM

OWFFF!

RUMMBBLLLLEEE

DEAR LADY!...WHAT HAVE YOU DONE?

OH! MY ANKLE!

NO...NO, DON'T TRY TO WALK.

I FEAR YOUR MODESTY DECLINES THAT WHICH YOUR SITUATION RENDERS NECESSARY.

PLEASE, PERMIT ME--

T-THAT IS M-MY HOME, THE GRAY COTTAGE D-DOWN THERE.

REST EASY NOW. I'LL SEE YOU SAFELY RETURNED TO YOUR FAMILY.

I AM MOST SORRY FOR THE INTRUSION, MA'AM, BUT YOUR DAUGHTER TOOK QUITE A TUMBLE.

I BELIEVE SHE HAS WRENCHED HER ANKLE.

WILL YOU TAKE A SEAT, SIR, WHILE I ATTEND HER?

WORDS CANNOT CONVEY HOW VERY GRATEFUL I AM FOR YOUR KIND ATTENTION TO MY DAUGHTER.

I AM WET THROUGH AND ALREADY DRIPPING MUD ON YOUR CARPET.

THEN AT LEAST TELL ME TO WHOM WE DASHWOODS ARE OBLIGED.

MY NAME IS WILLOUGHBY AND AT PRESENT I AM STAYING IN ALLENHAM.

I HOPE THAT YOU WILL ALLOW ME THE HONOR OF CALLING TOMORROW TO ENQUIRE AFTER MISS DASHWOOD.

CERTAINLY YOU MAY.

ONCE WILLOUGHBY DEPARTED...

WHAT A CHARMING AND PERSONABLE YOUNG MAN!

HE CARRIED MARIANNE WITH SO LITTLE EFFORT!

YES, QUITE A PARAGON OF MANLY ATTRIBUTES!

WHAT DID YOU THINK OF HIM, MY DEAR?

MY SITUATION WAS SO MORTIFYING... I BARELY REGARDED HIM AT FIRST.

YET I AM NOW CONVINCED HIS PERSON AND HIS AIR WERE...MY EXACT NOTION OF WHAT A PROPER HERO OUGHT TO BE.

UPON HEARING OF MARIANNE'S ACCIDENT, SIR JOHN RODE OVER LATER THAT DAY.

WILLOUGHBY, YOU SAY? BACK IN THE NEIGHBORHOOD? THAT'S HAPPY NEWS.

YOU KNOW HIM THEN?

HE'S DOWN HERE EVERY YEAR TO VISIT THE OLD LADY IN ALLENHAM COURT.

BUT WHAT DO YOU KNOW OF HIM?

HE'S A DECENT SHOT AND A BOLD RIDER.

HAS A PRETTY LITTLE ESTATE IN SOMERSET AND IS ALSO TO INHERIT ALLENHAM COURT WHEN THE OLD LADY PASSES ON.

YES, I BELIEVE HE IS WELL WORTH CATCHING.

MISS DASHWOOD, I WOULD NOT GIVE HIM UP TO YOUR SISTER, IN SPITE OF ALL THIS TUMBLING DOWN HILLS.

MARIANNE CAN'T EXPECT TO HAVE ALL THE YOUNG MEN TO HERSELF.

CATCHING MEN IS NOT AN EMPLOYMENT TO WHICH MY DAUGHTERS HAVE BEEN BROUGHT UP, SIR JOHN.

I AM GLAD TO FIND, HOWEVER, THAT HE IS A RESPECTABLE YOUNG MAN.

AYE, WILLOUGHBY IS AS GOOD A KIND OF FELLOW AS EVER LIVED.

IS THAT ALL YOU CAN SAY?

WHAT ARE HIS TALENTS, HIS PURSUITS, HIS GENIUS?

UPON MY SOUL, I DON'T KNOW SO MUCH ABOUT HIM AS THAT. HE DOES HAVE A FINE, BLACK POINTER...

AND I RECALL LAST CHRISTMAS, WHEN HE DANCED AT A BALL TILL DAWN AND WAS UP AGAIN AT EIGHT TO RIDE TO COVERT.

THAT IS WHAT A YOUNG MAN OUGHT TO BE.

WHATEVER HIS PURSUITS, HIS EAGERNESS IN THEM SHOULD KNOW NO MODERATION AND LEAVE HIM NO SENSE OF FATIGUE.

AH, I SEE HOW IT WILL BE.

YOU WILL BE SETTING YOUR CAP AT HIM NOW AND NEVER A THOUGHT FOR POOR BRANDON.

THAT IS AN EXPRESSION I PARTICULARLY DISLIKE.

I ABHOR EVERY COMMONPLACE PHRASE BY WHICH WIT IS INTENDED, BUT *"SETTING ONE'S CAP"* AND *"MAKING A CONQUEST"* ARE THE MOST ODIOUS OF ALL.

YET YOU WILL MAKE CONQUESTS ENOUGH, I DARESAY, ONE WAY OR THE OTHER.

BRANDON IS ALREADY SMITTEN AND IS WELL WORTH SETTING YOUR CAP AT, I CAN TELL YOU.

Mr. Willoughby called the next morning and was received with much more than politeness.

I DO ENJOY WALTER SCOTT IMMENSELY. I KNOW EVERYONE ESTEEMS *WAVERLY*, BUT MY OWN PARTICULAR FAVORITE IS--

ROB ROY? AH, THEN WE ARE IN AGREEMENT ON THAT SCORE, MISS MARIANNE. AND WHAT OF POETRY?

BYRON AND SHAKESPEARE'S SONNETS, OF COURSE, BUT MOST ESPECIALLY POPE.

YE FLOWERS THAT DROP, FORSAKEN BY THE SPRING, YE BIRDS THAT, LEFT BY SUMMER, CEASE TO SING,

YE TREES THAT FADE, WHEN AUTUMN HEATS REMOVE. SAY, IS NOT ABSENCE DEATH TO THOSE WHO LOVE?

AFTER MR. WILLOUGHBY TOOK HIS LEAVE...

FOR **ONE** MORNING I THINK YOU HAVE DONE PRETTY WELL.

YOU HAVE ASCERTAINED MR. WILLOUGHBY'S OPINION IN ALMOST EVERY MATTER OF IMPORTANCE.

BUT HOW, I WONDER, IS YOUR ACQUAINTANCE TO BE LONG SUPPORTED WHEN YOU HAVE EXHAUSTED EACH FAVORITE TOPIC?

ANOTHER VISIT WILL SUFFICE TO EXPLAIN HIS SENTIMENTS ON PICTURESQUE BEAUTY AND SECOND MARRIAGES, AND THEN YOU CAN HAVE NOTHING FURTHER TO ASK.

ELINOR, IS THIS FAIR? ARE MY IDEAS SO SCANTY?

BUT PERHAPS I HAVE ERRED AGAINST ALL COMMON NOTIONS OF DECORUM, BEEN TOO AT EASE, TOO FRANK.

I HAVE BEEN OPEN AND SINCERE WHERE I SHOULD HAVE BEEN SPIRITLESS, DULL, AND DECEITFUL.

IF I HAD SPOKEN ONLY OF THE WEATHER AND THE STATE OF THE ROADS, AND AT THAT ONLY ONCE EVERY TEN MINUTES, I SHOULD HAVE BEEN SPARED THIS REPROACH.

MARIANNE, YOUR SISTER SPOKE IN JEST.

SHE HAS NO WISH TO CHECK YOUR DELIGHT IN YOUR NEW FRIEND.

TRULY, I DON'T.

WILLOUGHBY CAME DAILY TO INQUIRE AFTER MARIANNE'S HEALTH, BUT SOON NEEDED NO EXCUSE FOR VISITING BARTON COTTAGE...

ONCE MARIANNE RECOVERED, SHE FOUND IN HIM HER PERFECT COUNTERPART...

LET BUCKS AND LET BLOODS TO PRAISE LONDON AGREE

OH THE JOYS OF THE COUNTRY MY JEWEL FOR ME

AND HOW CHARMING TO GATHER IT BUT FOR THE THORNS

WHERE SWEET'R IS THE FLOW'R THAT THE MAY BUSH ADORNS,

HE LEFT A CORSAIR'S NAME TO OTHER TIMES, LINKED WITH ONE VIRTUE, AND A THOUSAND CRIMES.

AND HIS SOCIETY QUICKLY BECAME HER MOST EXQUISITE ENJOYMENT.

I VOW, I CAN FIND NO FAULT WITH HIM.

YES, HE RESEMBLES MARIANNE IN EVERY PARTICULAR...

EVEN TO SAYING WHAT HE THINKS ON ALL OCCASIONS WITHOUT ATTENTION TO PERSONS OR CIRCUMSTANCES.

IF HE DOES SOMETIMES SACRIFICE POLITENESS, I DARESAY IT IS BECAUSE HE SEEKS THE UNDIVIDED ATTENTION OF THE ONE WHO HAS ENGAGED HIS HEART.

YET HE SO EASILY SLIGHTS THE FORMS OF WORLDLY PROPRIETY.

I FEAR THERE IS AT TIMES A WANT OF CAUTION...IN BOTH OF THEM.

NONSENSE. THEY ARE MERELY DISPLAYING THE HIGH SPIRITS OF YOUTH.

AH, I NEVER THOUGHT TO CONGRATULATE MYSELF ON GAINING TWO SUCH SONS-IN-LAW AS EDWARD FERRARS AND JOHN WILLOUGHBY.

AS THE GENERAL ATTENTION WAS DRAWN TO HIS MORE FORTUNATE RIVAL, BRANDON'S FEELINGS FOR MARIANNE BECAME MORE PERCEPTIBLE TO ELINOR.

YOUR SISTER, I GATHER, DOES NOT APPROVE OF SECOND ATTACHMENTS.

NO, HER OPINIONS ARE PURELY ROMANTIC ON THAT SCORE.

OR, RATHER, SHE CONSIDERS THEM IMPOSSIBLE TO EXIST.

I EXPECT THAT A FEW YEARS WILL SETTLE HER OPINIONS ON THE REASONABLE BASIS OF COMMON SENSE AND OBSERVATION.

I ONCE KNEW A LADY WHO IN TEMPER AND MIND RESEMBLED YOUR SISTER.

BUT WHO SUFFERED FROM AN ENFORCED CHANGE, FROM A SERIES OF UNFORTUNATE CIRCUMSTANCES...

IF YOU WILL EXCUSE ME, MISS DASHWOOD. I SPY AN OLD ACQUAINTANCE ACROSS THE ROOM...

EVEN SIR JOHN COULD NOT HELP REMARKING ON HIS FRIEND'S MELANCHOLY.

POOR CHAP. HE'S ALREADY HAD HIS SHARE OF PAST INJURIES AND DISAPPOINTMENTS.

I DON'T THINK... AH...

NO MIND, MISS DASHWOOD.

YOU MAY BE SURE THE FINE ANGLING IN MY TROUT STREAM WILL DISTRACT HIM.

BRANDON IS JUST THE KIND OF MAN WHOM EVERYBODY SPEAKS WELL OF, AND NOBODY CARES ABOUT; WHOM ALL ARE DELIGHTED TO SEE, AND NOBODY REMEMBERS TO TALK TO.

THAT IS EXACTLY WHAT I THINK OF HIM.

DO NOT BOAST OF IT, FOR IT IS AN INJUSTICE IN BOTH OF YOU.

HE IS HIGHLY ESTEEMED BY THE FAMILY AT THE PARK--

AH, BUT WHO WOULD SUBMIT TO THE INDIGNITY OF BEING APPROVED BY LADY MIDDLETON AND MRS. JENNINGS?

AND I NEVER SEE HIM WITHOUT TAKING PAINS TO CONVERSE WITH HIM.

HE HAS SEEN A GREAT DEAL OF THE WORLD; HAS BEEN ABROAD, HAS READ, AND HAS A THINKING MIND.

I DON'T KNOW WHY YOU SHOULD DISLIKE HIM.

THAT HE IS PATRONIZED BY YOU IS CERTAINLY IN HIS FAVOR.

AND I DO NOT DISLIKE HIM. ON THE CONTRARY I CONSIDER HIM A RESPECTABLE MAN WHO HAS EVERYBODY'S GOOD WORD...

AND NOBODY'S NOTICE.

YOU DECIDE ON HIS IMPERFECTIONS SO MUCH IN THE MASS, AND SO MUCH ON THE STRENGTH OF YOUR IMAGINATIONS, THAT MY COMMENDATION OF HIM IS COMPARATIVELY COLD AND INSIPID.

I CONFESS HIS CHARACTER TO BE IRREPROACHABLE--SAVE THAT HE FOUND FAULT WITH MY CURRICLE AND WILL NOT BUY MY BROWN MARE.

AND IN RETURN FOR THAT ACKNOWLEDGEMENT, YOU CANNOT DENY ME THE PRIVILEGE OF DISLIKING HIM AS MUCH AS EVER.

WILLOUGHBY HAS GIVEN ME A HORSE, A LADY'S MOUNT... HE BRED HER HIMSELF IN SOMERSET.

WHEN SHE ARRIVES YOU SHALL SHARE HER WITH ME.

YOU KNOW I WOULD LOVE NOTHING MORE. BUT WHAT OF THE COST OF FEEDING HER?

HOW SHALL WE EMPLOY A GROOM? MAMA CAN ILL AFFORD SUCH A THING.

VERY WELL, I WILL TELL WILLOUGHBY HIS KIND OFFER MUST BE DECLINED.

OH, ELINOR, I HAVE SUCH A SECRET TO TELL YOU!

I BELIEVE MARIANNE WILL BE MARRIED TO MR. WILLOUGHBY VERY SOON.

AND SO YOU HAVE SAID ALMOST EVERY DAY SINCE THEY MEET ON HIGH-CHURCH DOWN.

I AM QUITE SURE THIS TIME, FOR HE HAS GOT A LOCK OF HER HAIR.

TAKE... TAKE CARE, MARGARET.

IT MIGHT SIMPLY BE A LOCK FROM SOME GREAT UNCLE OR OTHER.

I SAW HIM TAKE IT. LAST NIGHT, AFTER TEA.

YOU AND MAMA WENT FROM THE ROOM, AND THEY WERE WHISPERING AND ARGUING, HE SEEMED TO BE BEGGING HER FOR SOME FAVOR...

AND PRESENTLY, HE TOOK UP HER SCISSORS AND CUT A LONG LOCK OF HER HAIR.

HE KISSED IT AND FOLDED IT INTO A WHITE PAPER AND PUT IT INTO HIS POCKET.

YOU MUST NOT TELL ANYONE, HOWEVER.

IT WILL REMAIN OUR SECRET.

YET THE VERY NEXT DAY IN THE MIDDLETON'S PARLOR, MARGARET FOUND HERSELF PRESSED TO REVEAL A CONFIDENCE OF A DIFFERENT SORT.

PRAY, TELL ME MARGARET, WHO IS MISS ELINOR'S PARTICULAR FAVORITE BEAU?

FOR I CONFESS THIS MATTER HAS LONG BEEN OF GREAT CURIOSITY TO ME.

I MUST NOT TELL, MAY I, ELINOR?

WHATEVER YOUR CONJECTURES MAY BE, MARGARET, YOU HAVE NO RIGHT TO REPEAT THEM.

I NEVER HAD ANY CONJECTURES. IT WAS YOU WHO TOLD ME OF IT.

OH, PLEASE... LET US ALL KNOW. WHAT IS THE MYSTERIOUS GENTLEMAN'S NAME?

YOU KNOW THIS IS AN INVENTION OF YOUR OWN, MARGARET, AND THERE IS NO SUCH PERSON IN EXISTENCE.

THEN HE IS LATELY DEAD, MARIANNE, FOR I AM SURE THERE WAS SUCH A MAN ONCE.

AND HIS NAME BEGINS WITH AN F.

ELINOR WAS GREATLY RELIEVED WHEN LADY MIDDLETON OBSERVED...

IT APPEARS TO BE RAINING QUITE HARD.

...THUS ENDING MRS. JENNINGS'S INQUISITION.

A WEEK LATER, COLONEL BRANDON ARRANGED A VISIT TO HIS BROTHER-IN-LAW WHO LIVED IN WHITWELL, A PARTICULARLY FINE HOUSE SOME TWELVE MILES DISTANT.

THE PARTY WAS ASSEMBLED AT THE PARK FOR BREAKFAST, WHEN THE COLONEL RECEIVED A MESSAGE.

NOT BAD NEWS, I HOPE.

MERELY A LETTER OF BUSINESS...FROM TOWN.

YET YOU ARE SO DISCOMPOSED. I FANCY I KNOW WHO IT IS FROM.

AND I HOPE SHE IS WELL.

I REGRET THAT I SHOULD RECEIVE THIS LETTER TODAY. IT REQUIRES MY IMMEDIATE ATTENDANCE IN TOWN.

I FEAR WE MUST PUT OFF OUR TRIP TO WHITWELL FOR ANOTHER DAY. I CANNOT LOSE ONE HOUR.

WHOM DO YOU MEAN?

OH, YOU KNOW WHO I MEAN.

IS THERE A CHANCE I MIGHT SEE YOU AND YOUR SISTERS IN LONDON THIS WINTER?

NONE AT ALL, I'M AFRAID.

THEN I MUST BID YOU FAREWELL FOR LONGER THAN I WISH TO.

THERE ARE SOME PEOPLE WHO CANNOT BEAR A PARTY OF PLEASURE.

HE WAS AFRAID OF CATCHING COLD I DARE SAY.

I CAN GUESS WHAT THIS BUSINESS IS ABOUT.

MISS WILLIAMS, OF COURSE. A NEAR RELATION OF THE COLONEL'S.

THOUGH HOW NEAR, I CANNOT SAY FOR FEAR OF SHOCKING THE LADIES.

HIS NATURAL DAUGHTER. AS LIKE HIM AS SHE CAN STARE.

IT IS EXPECTED HE WILL LEAVE HIS FORTUNE TO HER.

*S*IR JOHN SUGGESTED THAT RATHER THAN WASTING THE DAY, HIS GUESTS SHOULD TAKE ADVANTAGE OF THE FINE WEATHER BY DRIVING ABOUT THE COUNTRYSIDE.

I WAGER THEY'LL BE OUT OF THE DRIVE AND LOST FROM SIGHT BEFORE WE ARE EVEN SEATED IN OUR CARRIAGE.

LATER THAT EVENING, SIR JOHN ARRANGED AN INFORMAL DINNER PARTY FOR HIS GUESTS.

SLY PUSS, IN SPITE OF YOUR TRICKS, I KNOW WHERE YOU SPENT THE MORNING.

YOU KNOW QUITE WELL WE WERE OUT IN MY CURRICLE.

AH, BUT *WHERE* DID IT TAKE YOU, MR. IMPUDENCE?

MISS MARIANNE, I HOPE YOU LIKE *YOUR* HOUSE...

IT IS A VERY LARGE ONE AND I TRUST WHEN I COME SEE YOU THERE, YOU WILL HAVE IT NEWLY FURNISHED.

ONCE THEY WERE BACK AT THE COTTAGE, ELINOR PRESSED HER SISTER FOR AN EXPLANATION.

SO IS IT TRUE WHAT LADY JENNINGS SAID? YOU VISITED ALLENHAM COURT?

IS IT NOT WHAT YOU HAVE WISHED TO DO YOURSELF?

YES, BUT CERTAINLY NOT WHILE MRS. SMITH WAS UPSTAIRS ABED...

AND WITH NO COMPANION BUT WILLOUGHBY.

WILLOUGHBY IS THE ONLY PERSON WHO HAS A RIGHT TO SHOW ME THE HOUSE.

THERE COULD BE NO IMPROPRIETY OR I SHOULD HAVE BEEN SENSIBLE OF IT AT THE TIME, FOR WE ALWAYS KNOW WHEN WE ARE ACTING WRONG.

YET IT HAS ALREADY EXPOSED YOU TO SEVERAL IMPERTINENT REMARKS. DO YOU STILL NOT DOUBT THE DISCRETION OF YOUR CONDUCT?

I HAVE DONE NOTHING WRONG IN WALKING OVER MRS. SMITH'S GROUNDS OR SEEING HER HOUSE. THEY WILL ONE DAY BE WILLOUGHBY'S--

IF THEY WERE ONE DAY TO BE YOUR *OWN*, MARIANNE, YOU CANNOT BE JUSTIFIED IN WHAT YOU HAVE DONE!

YOU KNOW I AM RIGHT.

I KNOW NOTHING OF THE KIND.

BARELY A HALF HOUR LATER...

PERHAPS IT *WAS* ILL-JUDGED OF ME TO GO, BUT WILLOUGHBY *PARTICULARLY* WANTED ME TO SEE IT.

I...I WAS QUITE TAKEN BY ONE PRETTY SITTING ROOM, THOUGH THE FURNITURE WAS SADLY FORLORN.

WILLOUGHBY SAYS A FEW HUNDRED POUNDS WOULD...M-MAKE IT THE PLEASANTEST SUMMER-ROOM IN ENGLAND.

WHEN WILLOUGHBY CALLED THE NEXT MORNING, MRS. DASHWOOD MOTIONED HIM TO HER SIDE IN THE PARLOR.

COME, YOU MUST SEE MY SKETCHES FOR THE NEW ADDITION TO OUR COTTAGE.

WHAT! IMPROVE THIS DEAR COTTAGE!

NO, *THAT* I WOULD NEVER CONSENT TO.

NOT A STONE MUST BE ADDED TO ITS WALLS, NOT AN INCH TO ITS SIZE.

DO NOT BE ALARMED. MY MOTHER WILL NEVER HAVE MONEY ENOUGH TO ATTEMPT IT.

I AM HEARTILY GLAD OF IT. THIS PLACE WILL ALWAYS HAVE ONE CLAIM ON MY AFFECTION...

...WHICH NONE OTHER CAN SHARE.

THE FOLLOWING DAY, MRS. DASHWOOD AND HER TWO DAUGHTERS CAME HOME FROM A WALK TO FIND WILLOUGHBY'S CURRICLE IN THE DRIVE.

GOOD HEAVENS! WHAT'S HAPPENED?

MARIANNE... PLEASE, WHAT IS WRONG?

IS ANYTHING THE MATTER WITH MARIANNE? IS SHE ILL?

I HOPE NOT. IT IS I WHO MAY EXPECT TO BE ILL.

MRS. SMITH HAS, THIS VERY MORNING, EXERCISED THE PRIVILEGE OF RICHES UPON A DEPENDANT COUSIN BY SENDING ME TO LONDON ON BUSINESS.

I HAVE TAKEN MY LEAVE OF ALLENHAM AND AM NOW COME TO TAKE MY FAREWELL OF YOU.

TO LONDON! ARE YOU GOING THIS MORNING?

ALMOST AT THIS MOMENT.

BUT SURELY YOUR BUSINESS WILL NOT DETAIN YOU FROM US FOR LONG.

ALAS, MY VISITS TO MRS. SMITH ARE NEVER REPEATED WITHIN THE TWELVEMONTH.

I...I WILL NOT TORMENT MYSELF ANY LONGER BY REMAINING AMONG FRIENDS WHOSE SOCIETY IT IS NOW IMPOSSIBLE FOR ME TO ENJOY.

BARTON COTTAGE, DEVON, LATE AUTUMN.

IN HER GRIEF OVER WILLOUGHBY'S DEPARTURE, MARIANNE WEPT ALL THROUGH THE NIGHT...

AND THE NEXT DAY REVISITED EVERY PIECE OF MUSIC SHE AND WILLOUGHBY HAD SHARED AT THE PIANOFORTE, ALTERNATELY SINGING AND CRYING.

HER MOTHER AND SISTER COULD HARDLY REMAIN UNAWARE OF HER DISTRESS.

YOU MUST KNOW THAT I DO NOT BLAME WILLOUGHBY. I AM PERSUADED MRS. SMITH SUSPECTED HIS REGARD FOR MARIANNE AND INVENTED AN EXCUSE TO SEND HIM FROM THE DISTRICT.

HE IS, I AM CONVINCED, AWARE OF HER DISAPPROVAL OF THE CONNECTION AND SO DARED NOT CONFESS THEIR ENGAGEMENT. AND IN LIGHT OF HIS DEPENDANT SITUATION, HE HAS ABSENTED HIMSELF FROM DEVON FOR A WHILE.

NOW YOU MAY TELL ME THAT THIS IS NOT WHAT HAS HAPPENED, BUT I WILL LISTEN TO NO OBJECTION. WHAT SAY YOU, ELINOR?

NOTHING. YOU HAVE ANTICIPATED MY ANSWER.

OH, HARSH ELINOR. YOU HAD RATHER LOOK OUT FOR MISERY FOR MARIANNE AND GUILT FOR POOR WILLOUGHBY, THAN AN APOLOGY FOR THE LATTER.

YOU ARE RESOLVED TO THINK HIM AT FAULT. IS NOTHING DUE TO THE MAN WHOM WE HAVE SUCH REASON TO LOVE AND NO REASON IN THE WORLD TO THINK ILL OF?

SUSPICION OF SOMETHING UNPLEASANT IS THE INEVITABLE CONSEQUENCE OF SUCH AN ALTERATION AS WE WITNESSED IN HIM YESTERDAY.

FURTHERMORE, IT MAY BE PROPER TO CONCEAL THEIR ENGAGEMENT FROM MRS. SMITH...BUT THERE IS NO EXCUSE FOR THEIR CONCEALING IT FROM US.

DO YOU ACCUSE THEM OF CONCEALMENT, WHEN FOR DAYS YOUR EYES HAVE BEEN REPROACHING THEM FOR INCAUTIOUSNESS?

I WANT NO PROOF OF THEIR AFFECTION, BUT OF THEIR ENGAGEMENT I DO.

I AM PERFECTLY SATISFIED OF BOTH.

HAS NOT HIS BEHAVIOR TO MARIANNE DECLARED THAT HE LOVED HER AND CONSIDERED HER AS HIS FUTURE WIFE?

HAS NOT MY CONSENT BEEN ASKED DAILY BY HIS LOOKS AND MANNER, HIS ATTENTIVE AND AFFECTIONATE RESPECT?

EVERY CIRCUMSTANCE BUT ONE IS IN FAVOR OF THEIR ENGAGEMENT, BUT THAT ONE IS THE TOTAL SILENCE OF BOTH ON THE SUBJECT.

WITH ME IT OUTWEIGHS EVERY OTHER.

*O*NE EVENING A FEW DAYS LATER, MRS. DASHWOOD ABSENTLY PICKED UP A VOLUME OF SHAKESPEARE...

WE HAVE NEVER FINISHED HAMLET, MARIANNE. OUR DEAR WILLOUGHBY WENT AWAY BEFORE WE COULD GET THROUGH IT.

WE WILL PUT IT BY FOR WHEN HE COMES AGAIN. THOUGH THAT MAY BE MONTHS...

MONTHS! NO--NOR MANY WEEKS.

THIS SMALL EXCHANGE PLEASED ELINOR, ELICITING AS IT DID FROM MARIANNE AN EXPRESSION OF CONFIDENCE IN WILLOUGHBY AND KNOWLEDGE OF HIS INTENTIONS.

A WEEK AFTER WILLOUGHBY'S DEPARTURE, MARIANNE AT LAST REJOINED HER SISTERS FOR THEIR DAILY WALK UPON THE MOORS.

LOOK!

IT IS HE! INDEED, I KNOW IT IS!

I THINK YOU ARE MISTAKEN. IT IS NOT WILLOUGHBY. THE GENTLEMAN IS NOT TALL ENOUGH, AND HAS NOT HIS AIR.

HE HAS, HE HAS. HIS AIR, HIS COAT, HIS HORSE. I KNEW HOW SOON HE WOULD COME!

YOU WERE RIGHT. IT IS NOT WILLOUGHBY.

YET IT WAS, PERHAPS, THE ONE MAN MARIANNE COULD FORGIVE FOR NOT BEING WILLOUGHBY-- EDWARD FERRARS.

PLEASE STOP, MISS MARIANNE. WHY DO YOU TURN AWAY?

MR. FERRARS! I DID NOT RECOGNIZE YOU AT FIRST.

HOW...HOW WONDERFUL THAT YOU HAVE COME TO VISIT US.

HAVE YOU COME DIRECTLY FROM LONDON?

NO, I HAVE BEEN IN DEVON A FORTNIGHT...

A FORTNIGHT?

I'VE BEEN STAYING WITH SOME FRIENDS IN PLYMOUTH. AND I WAS AT NORLAND BEFORE THAT.

AND HOW DOES DEAR NORLAND LOOK? ARE THE WOODLANDS THICKLY COATED WITH DEAD LEAVES?

HOW I DELIGHTED TO WALK THROUGH THEM AND SEE THEM DRIVEN IN SHOWERS ABOUT ME BY THE WIND.

NOT EVERYONE HAS YOUR PASSION FOR DEAD LEAVES.

NO, MY FEELINGS ARE NOT OFTEN SHARED. BUT *SOMETIMES* THEY ARE.

NOW, EDWARD, HERE IS BARTON VALLEY. DID YOU EVER SEE THE EQUAL OF THOSE HILLS?

IT IS BEAUTIFUL COUNTRY, BUT THESE LANES MUST BE DIRTY IN WINTER.

HOW CAN YOU THINK OF DIRT WITH SUCH OBJECTS BEFORE YOU?

BECAUSE, AMONG THE REST OF THE OBJECTS BEFORE ME, I SEE A VERY DIRTY LANE.

HAVE YOU AN AGREEABLE NEIGHBORHOOD HERE? ARE THE MIDDLETONS PLEASANT PEOPLE?

NO, NOT AT ALL. WE COULDN'T BE MORE UNFORTUNATELY SITUATED.

MARIANNE! HOW CAN YOU BE SO INJUST? THEY HAVE BEHAVED TOWARDS US IN THE FRIENDLIEST MANNER, MR. FERRARS.

HAVE YOU FORGOT, MARIANNE, HOW MANY PLEASANT DAYS WE OWE TO THEM?

NO, NOR HOW MANY PAINFUL MOMENTS.

ELINOR DIRECTED HER ATTENTION TOWARD EDWARD, ENDEAVORING TO TALK TO HIM OF THEIR PRESENT RESIDENCE AND ITS CONVENIENCES, BUT WAS MET WITH A CERTAIN COLDNESS.

SHE WAS MORTIFIED AND A LITTLE VEXED BY HIS RESERVE.

EDWARD, MY DEAR BOY. WHAT A DELIGHTFUL SURPRISE!

COME IN... BY ALL MEANS COME IN. I'LL RING FOR TEA.

SO, EDWARD, WHAT ARE YOUR MOTHER'S VIEWS FOR YOU?

ARE YOU STILL DESTINED TO BECOME A GREAT ORATOR IN SPITE OF YOURSELF?

I HOPE MY MOTHER IS NOW CONVINCED THAT I HAVE NO MORE TALENTS THAN INCLINATION FOR PUBLIC LIFE. I HAVE NO WISH TO BE DISTINGUISHED AND NO HOPE TO BE.

I WISH AS MUCH AS EVERY BODY ELSE TO BE HAPPY, BUT LIKE EVERY BODY ELSE, IT MUST BE IN MY OWN WAY. GREATNESS WILL NOT MAKE ME SO.

I SHOULD THINK NOT. WHAT HAVE WEALTH OR GRANDEUR TO DO WITH HAPPINESS?

GRANDEUR HAS LITTLE, BUT WEALTH HAS MUCH TO DO WITH IT.

A PROPER ESTABLISHMENT-- WITH SERVANTS, TWO CARRIAGES, A FEW HUNTERS--COULD NOT BE SUPPORTED FOR LESS.

ELINOR, FOR SHAME! MONEY CAN ONLY GIVE HAPPINESS WHEN THERE IS NOTHING ELSE TO GIVE IT. I KNOW I COULD LIVE VERY COMFORTABLY ON ONLY TWO THOUSAND A YEAR.

AH...I WONDER IF SHE KNOWS SHE HAS QUITE ACCURATELY DESCRIBED HER FUTURE EXPENSES FOR RUNNING WILLOUGHBY'S HOME, COMBE MAGNA.

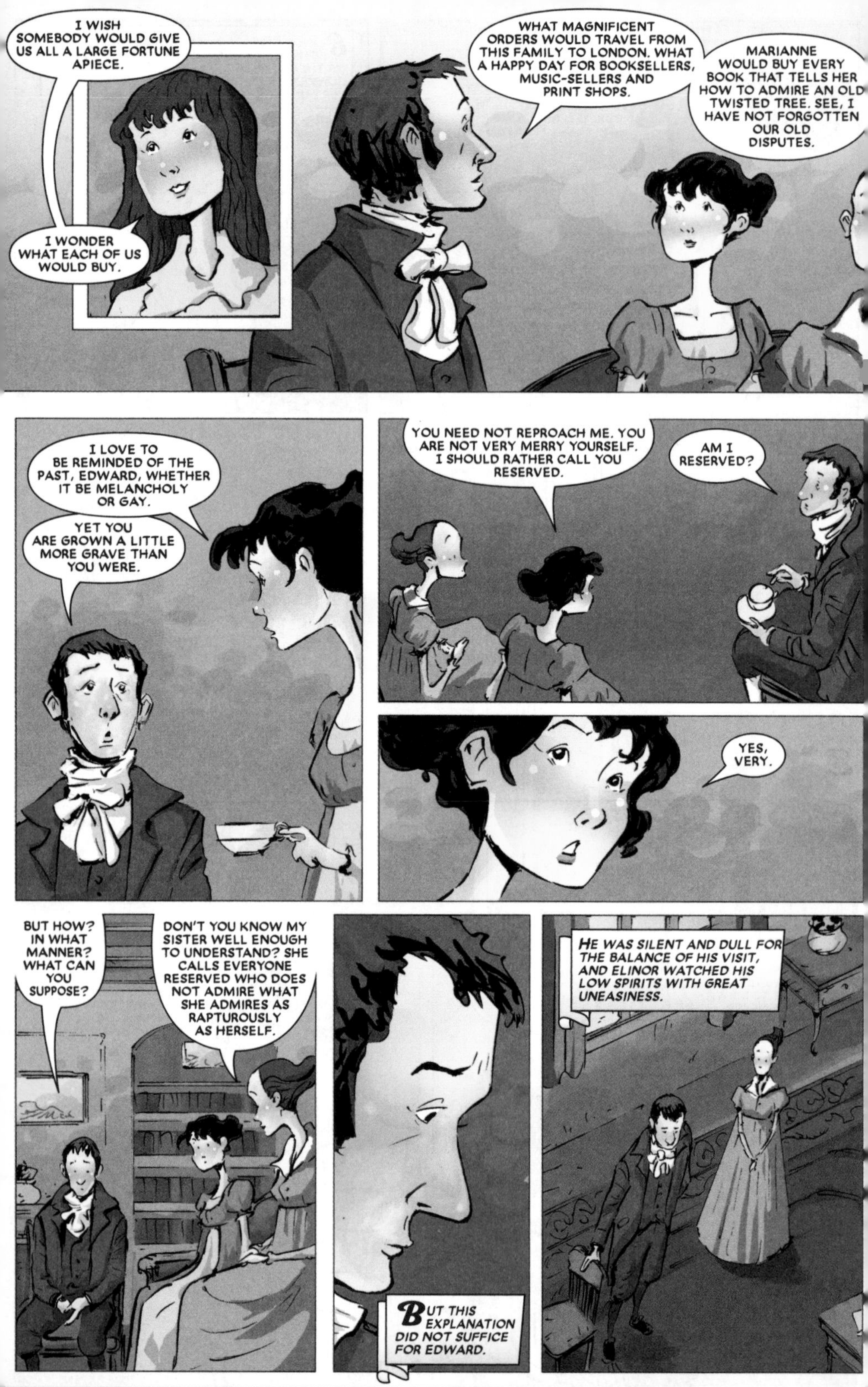
I WISH SOMEBODY WOULD GIVE US ALL A LARGE FORTUNE APIECE.
I WONDER WHAT EACH OF US WOULD BUY.
WHAT MAGNIFICENT ORDERS WOULD TRAVEL FROM THIS FAMILY TO LONDON. WHAT A HAPPY DAY FOR BOOKSELLERS, MUSIC-SELLERS AND PRINT SHOPS.
MARIANNE WOULD BUY EVERY BOOK THAT TELLS HER HOW TO ADMIRE AN OLD TWISTED TREE. SEE, I HAVE NOT FORGOTTEN OUR OLD DISPUTES.
I LOVE TO BE REMINDED OF THE PAST, EDWARD, WHETHER IT BE MELANCHOLY OR GAY.
YET YOU ARE GROWN A LITTLE MORE GRAVE THAN YOU WERE.
YOU NEED NOT REPROACH ME. YOU ARE NOT VERY MERRY YOURSELF. I SHOULD RATHER CALL YOU RESERVED.
AM I RESERVED?
YES, VERY.
BUT HOW? IN WHAT MANNER? WHAT CAN YOU SUPPOSE?
DON'T YOU KNOW MY SISTER WELL ENOUGH TO UNDERSTAND? SHE CALLS EVERYONE RESERVED WHO DOES NOT ADMIRE WHAT SHE ADMIRES AS RAPTUROUSLY AS HERSELF.
BUT THIS EXPLANATION DID NOT SUFFICE FOR EDWARD.
HE WAS SILENT AND DULL FOR THE BALANCE OF HIS VISIT, AND ELINOR WATCHED HIS LOW SPIRITS WITH GREAT UNEASINESS.

ON THE FINAL MORNING OF HIS VISIT, AS THE FAMILY WAS TAKING TEA...

I NEVER SAW YOU WEAR THAT RING, EDWARD. IS THAT FANNY'S HAIR? I SHOULD HAVE THOUGHT HER HAIR WOULD BE DARKER.

YES, YES... IT IS MY SISTER'S HAIR.

THE SETTING CASTS A DIFFERENT SHADE UPON IT.

COULD IT POSSIBLY BE A LOCK OF MY OWN HAIR? YET, AS I NEVER GAVE IT FREELY, HE MUST HAVE PROCURED IT BY SOME CONTRIVANCE.

I'VE BEEN THINKING, EDWARD THAT YOU WOULD BE A HAPPIER MAN IF YOU HAD A PROFESSION TO ENGAGE YOUR INTEREST.

YOU MIGHT NOT BE ABLE TO GIVE SO MUCH OF YOUR TIME TO YOUR FRIENDS, BUT YOU WOULD KNOW WHERE TO GO WHEN YOU LEFT THEM.

I HAVE THOUGHT LONG ON THIS POINT, AS YOU THINK NOW. BUT THE NICETY OF MY FRIENDS HAS MADE ME WHAT I AM, AN IDLE, HELPLESS BEING.

I ALWAYS PREFERRED THE CHURCH, BUT THAT WAS NOT SMART ENOUGH FOR MY FAMILY. THEY RECOMMENDED THE ARMY-- BUT THAT WAS A GREAT DEAL TOO SMART FOR ME.

COME, COME, YOU ARE IN A MELANCHOLY HUMOR. YOU WANT NOTHING BUT PATIENCE--OR TO GIVE IT A MORE FASCINATING NAME, CALL IT HOPE. YOUR MOTHER WILL SECURE TO YOU, IN TIME, THAT INDEPENDENCE YOU ARE SO ANXIOUS FOR.

IT IS HER DUTY AND ERE LONG WILL BECOME HER HAPPINESS TO PREVENT YOUR WHOLE YOUTH FROM BEING WASTED IN DISCONTENT. HOW MUCH MAY NOT A FEW MONTHS DO?

I THINK THAT I MAY DEFY MANY MONTHS TO PRODUCE ANY GOOD IN ME.

AND IN THAT DESPONDING STATE OF MIND, EDWARD DEPARTED FROM BARTON VALLEY.

ONCE HE WAS OUT OF VIEW, ELINOR SAT DOWN AT HER DRAWING TABLE AND BUSILY EMPLOYED HERSELF THE WHOLE DAY.

AND WHILE THIS CONDUCT DID NOT LESSEN HER OWN GRIEF, HER MOTHER AND SISTERS WERE SPARED MUCH SOLICITUDE ON HER ACCOUNT.

ELINOR WAS SO INWARDLY DISTRAUGHT, THAT AN UNEXPECTED VISIT FROM MRS. JENNINGS WAS ALMOST A WELCOME DIVERSION...

IMAGINE MY SURPRISE WHEN MY YOUNGEST DAUGHTER AND HER HUSBAND ARRIVED AT THE PARK LAST NIGHT. LET ME MAKE KNOWN TO YOU MR. PALMER AND MY DAUGHTER CHARLOTTE.

AH, BUT WHERE ARE YOUR SISTERS, ELINOR? OUT WALKING, I DARESAY. IT IS UNCOMMON WARM FOR NOVEMBER.

WHAT A DELIGHTFUL ROOM THIS IS! ONLY THINK, MAMA, HOW IT IS IMPROVED SINCE I WAS HERE LAST.

MRS. DASHWOOD, YOU HAVE MADE IT SO CHARMING! I SHOULD LIKE SUCH A HOUSE FOR MYSELF. SHOULD YOU NOT, MR. PALMER?

MR. PALMER DOES NOT HEAR ME. HE NEVER DOES SOMETIMES.

IT IS SO RIDICULOUS.

I URGED CHARLOTTE TO STAY HOME AND REST THIS MORNING, BUT SHE INSISTED ON COMING HERE TO VISIT YOU.

I DIDN'T SEE HOW A SHORT WALK WOULD DO ME ANY HARM.

SHE EXPECTS TO BE CONFINED IN FEBRUARY.

ER...THEN I MUST OFFER YOU MY CONGRATULATIONS, MRS. PALMER. AND YOU TOO, MR. PALMER.

WHAT? WHAT WAS THAT?

AUSTEN TIMES

LOOK, HERE COMES MARIANNE. NOW, MY DEARS, YOU SHALL SEE A MONSTROUS PRETTY GIRL.

DON'T HANG BACK, GIRLS. COME MEET MY DAUGHTER AND HER HUSBAND, WHO ARE VISITING FROM SOMERSET.

SOMERSET? HOW I HAVE LONGED TO SEE SOMERSET.

PERHAPS YOU COULD VISIT US THERE AT CLEVELAND SOME TIME. I CAN SEE THAT MR. PALMER IS ALSO QUITE TAKEN WITH THE IDEA.

As the tea tray came in, Mrs. Palmer took Elinor aside.

YOUR SISTER HAS LIVED UP TO MY MOTHER'S HIGH PRAISE. AND I MUST SAY I ADMIRE MARIANNE'S TASTE VERY MUCH, FOR I THINK MR. WILLOUGHBY QUITE HANDSOME--NOT THAT I EVER SPOKE TO HIM.

STILL, HIS HOME IS BUT THIRTY MILES FROM OUR OWN IN SOMERSET.

MRS. PALMER. I DON'T THINK--

I AM SO PLEASED YOUR SISTER IS TO MARRY HIM, FOR THEN I SHALL HAVE HER AS MY NEIGHBOR.

UPON MY WORD, YOU KNOW MORE OF THE MATTER THAN I DO, IF YOU HAVE REASON TO EXPECT SUCH A MATCH.

DON'T DENY IT, MY DEAR. IT IS ALL ANYONE TALKS OF.

WHY, COLONEL BRANDON AND I SPOKE OF IT JUST BEFORE I LEFT TOWN. I ASKED HIM IF IT WAS TRUE THAT WILLOUGHBY WAS TO BE MARRIED TO MISS MARIANNE, AND HE SAID...

WELL, HE GAVE ME SUCH A STRONG LOOK, AS IF HE KNEW IT TO BE TRUE.

Elinor felt only relief when their guests finally departed.

WHAT DELIGHTFUL DAUGHTERS YOU HAVE, MRS. DASHWOOD. WE SHALL LOOK FORWARD TO MEETING THEM AGAIN IN TOWN THIS WINTER.

WE WILL NOT BE GOING TO LONDON.

NOT GO TO TOWN! I SHALL BE QUITE DISAPPOINTED IF YOU DO NOT.

I COULD GET THE NICEST HOUSE FOR YOU, NEXT DOOR TO OURS IN HANOVER SQUARE.

MAMA, COULD WE NOT?

WE MUST DECLINE, I'M AFRAID.

WE LIVE A QUIET LIFE HERE AND ARE QUITE SATISFIED TO DO SO.

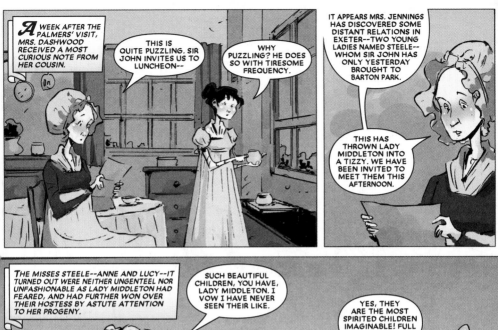

A WEEK AFTER THE PALMERS' VISIT, MRS. DASHWOOD RECEIVED A MOST CURIOUS NOTE FROM HER COUSIN.

THIS IS QUITE PUZZLING. SIR JOHN INVITES US TO LUNCHEON--

WHY PUZZLING? HE DOES SO WITH TIRESOME FREQUENCY.

IT APPEARS MRS. JENNINGS HAS DISCOVERED SOME DISTANT RELATIONS IN EXETER--TWO YOUNG LADIES NAMED STEELE-- WHOM SIR JOHN HAS ONLY YESTERDAY BROUGHT TO BARTON PARK.

THIS HAS THROWN LADY MIDDLETON INTO A TIZZY. WE HAVE BEEN INVITED TO MEET THEM THIS AFTERNOON.

THE MISSES STEELE--ANNE AND LUCY--IT TURNED OUT WERE NEITHER UNGENTEEL NOR UNFASHIONABLE AS LADY MIDDLETON HAD FEARED, AND HAD FURTHER WON OVER THEIR HOSTESS BY ASTUTE ATTENTION TO HER PROGENY.

SUCH BEAUTIFUL CHILDREN, YOU HAVE, LADY MIDDLETON. I VOW I HAVE NEVER SEEN THEIR LIKE.

YES, THEY ARE THE MOST SPIRITED CHILDREN IMAGINABLE! FULL OF MONKEY TRICKS.

AH, THIS MUST BE MRS. DASHWOOD AND HER DAUGHTERS.

HOW I HAVE LONGED TO MEET YOU, ELINOR AND MARIANNE.

JUST THEN THE YOUNGEST BOY BEGAN SCREAMING AND LADY MIDDLETON GATHERED THEM ALL UP AND DEPARTED.

HOW ARE YOU ENJOYING DEVON, MISS DASHWOOD? WERE YOU VERY SORRY TO LEAVE NORLAND?

AH, YOU KNOW OF OUR FORMER HOME?

WE HAVE HEARD SIR JOHN ADMIRE IT EXCESSIVELY. AND I SUPPOSE YOU HAD MANY SMART BEAUX IN SUSSEX.

I THINK THEY ARE A VAST ADDITION ALWAYS, PROVIDING THEY DRESS SMART AND BEHAVE CIVIL. I FEAR THERE ARE NOT MANY GENTEEL YOUNG MEN IN DEVONSHIRE.

LORD, ANNE, CAN YOU TALK OF NOTHING BUT BEAUX? YOU WILL MAKE MISS DASHWOOD BELIEVE YOU THINK OF LITTLE ELSE.

BUT SIR JOHN CONTINUED TO THROW HIS YOUNG RELATIONS TOGETHER, AND NEVER LEFT OFF TEASING ELINOR ABOUT HER MYSTERIOUS SUITOR AND THE LETTER "F."

I UNDERSTAND YOUR SISTER MADE A CONQUEST AFTER COMING TO BARTON.

TWILL BE A PRODIGIOUS THING TO HAVE HER MARRIED SO YOUNG. I HOPE YOU MAY HAVE AS MUCH LUCK YOURSELF SOON-- BUT PERHAPS YOU MAY HAVE A FRIEND IN THE CORNER ALREADY.

SIR JOHN HINTS TO US THAT HIS NAME IS FERRARS. YOU SISTER-IN-LAW'S BROTHER. A VERY AGREEABLE MAN, TO BE SURE. I KNOW HIM WELL.

HOW CAN YOU SAY SO, ANNE? WE HAVE ONLY SEEN HIM ONCE OR TWICE AT OUR UNCLE'S HOME.

PLEASE, PAY HER NO MIND, MISS DASHWOOD.

LATER THAT WEEK, LUCY INSISTED ON ACCOMPANYING ELINOR HOME FROM BARTON PARK.

YOU WILL THINK THIS AN ODD QUESTION, BUT HAVE YOU EVER MET YOUR SISTER-IN-LAW'S MOTHER, MRS. FERRARS? COULD YOU TELL ME WHAT SORT OF WOMAN SHE IS?

NO, I HAVE NOT MET HER AND KNOW NOTHING ABOUT HER.

PLEASE DON'T THINK ME STRANGE FOR ENQUIRING. I HAVE MY REASONS. I...

I CANNOT BEAR FOR YOU TO THINK ME IMPERTINENTLY CURIOUS. BUT I AM IN SUCH AN UNCOMFORTABLE SITUATION AND SHOULD BE GLAD OF YOUR ADVICE.

I AM NOT SURE HOW I COULD ADVISE YOU...SINCE I DO NOT KNOW MRS. FERRARS.

I NEVER HEARD THAT YOU WERE AT ALL CONNECTED TO THAT FAMILY, AND AM THEREFORE A LITTLE SURPRISED AT SO SERIOUS AN INQUIRY INTO HER CHARACTER.

NO DOUBT YOU ARE. BUT IF I DARED TO TELL YOU ALL, YOU WOULD NOT BE SO MUCH SURPRISED.

MRS. FERRARS IS NOTHING TO ME AT PRESENT. BUT THE TIME *MAY* COME-- HOW SOON IT WILL COME MUST DEPEND UPON HERSELF--WHEN WE MAY BE VERY INTIMATELY CONNECTED.

GOOD HEAVENS! ARE YOU ACQUAINTED WITH MR. ROBERT FERRARS? CAN YOU BE?

NO, NOT *ROBERT* FERRARS--I NEVER SAW HIM IN MY LIFE. I AM SPEAKING OF HIS ELDEST BROTHER.

I AM SURE YOU HAD NO WORD OF OUR ENGAGEMENT FROM *HIM*, NOT THE MEREST HINT. IT WAS ALWAYS MEANT TO BE A GREAT SECRET.

THOUGH MR. FERRARS CANNOT BE DISPLEASED THAT I TRUSTED YOU, BECAUSE I KNOW HE HAS THE HIGHEST REGARD FOR YOUR FAMILY...

...AND LOOKS UPON YOU AND THE OTHER MISS DASHWOODS AS HIS OWN SISTERS.

MAY I ASK IF THE ENGAGEMENT IS OF LONG STANDING?

WE HAVE BEEN ENGAGED THESE FOUR YEARS.

FOUR YEARS?

MR. FERRAR WAS MY UNCLE'S PUPIL AND LODGED WITH HIM IN PLYMOUTH FOR SEVERAL YEARS. IT WAS THERE WE MET.

AND ALTHOUGH YOU DO NOT KNOW HIM AS WELL AS I DO, YOU MUST HAVE SEEN THAT HE IS CAPABLE OF MAKING A WOMAN SINCERELY ATTACHED TO HIM.

CERTAINLY.

ENGAGED TO MR. EDWARD FERRARS! I CONFESS MYSELF TOTALLY SURPRISED. I BEG YOUR PARDON, BUT WE CANNOT MEAN THE SAME MR. FERRARS.

WE CAN MEAN NO OTHER. EDWARD FERRARS, ELDEST SON OF MRS. FERRARS OF PARK STREET. I AM NOT LIKELY TO BE DECEIVED AS TO THE NAME OF THE MAN ON WHO ALL MY HAPPINESS DEPENDS.

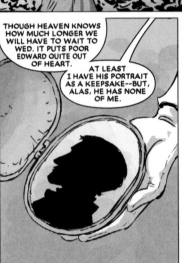

THOUGH HEAVEN KNOWS HOW MUCH LONGER WE WILL HAVE TO WAIT TO WED. IT PUTS POOR EDWARD QUITE OUT OF HEART.

AT LEAST I HAVE HIS PORTRAIT AS A KEEPSAKE--BUT, ALAS, HE HAS NONE OF ME.

I HAVE NO DOUBT IN THE WORLD OF YOUR FAITHFULLY KEEPING THIS SECRET.

I CERTAINLY DID NOT SEEK THIS CONFIDENCE...BUT YOUR SECRET IS SAFE WITH ME. I ONLY WONDER YOU SHARED IT, IF YOU FELT MY KNOWING IT COULD NOT ADD TO ITS SAFETY.

I REALLY THOUGHT SOME EXPLANATION WAS DUE TO YOU AFTER MAKING INQUIRIES ABOUT EDWARD'S MOTHER.

YOU SEE, I FEAR SHE WILL NOT APPROVE OF ME. I SHALL HAVE NO FORTUNE, AND I FANCY SHE IS AN EXCEEDINGLY PROUD WOMAN.

YOU CAN HAVE NO IDEA HOW I HAVE SUFFERED FOR EDWARD'S SAKE, EVERY THING IN SUCH SUSPENSE AND UNCERTAINTY. WE CAN HARDLY MEET ABOVE TWICE A YEAR.

DID...DID HE COME FROM YOUR UNCLE'S THEN, WHEN HE VISITED US?

YES, HE WAS WITH US A FORTNIGHT. HE WAS IN SUCH POOR SPIRITS, THOUGH, I GAVE HIM A LOCK OF MY HAIR TO SET IN A RING. PERHAPS YOU SAW IT?

I DID.

FORTUNATELY FOR ELINOR THEY HAD NOW REACHED THE COTTAGE GATE. LUCY TURNED BACK TOWARD THE PARK AND ELINOR WAS THEN AT LIBERTY TO THINK AND BE WRETCHED.

As ELINOR SORTED OUT HER FEELINGS, HER RESENTMENT AT BEING DUPED GAVE WAY TO A MORE RATIONAL CONSIDERATION OF EDWARD'S BEHAVIOR.

HAD HE INTENTIONALLY DECEIVED HER? HAD HE FEIGNED A REGARD HE DID NOT FEEL?

NO, HIS AFFECTION WAS ALL MY OWN. I AM NOT DECEIVED IN THAT. MY MOTHER, MY SISTERS--EVEN FANNY-- ALL WERE CONSCIOUS OF HIS REGARD FOR ME AT NORLAND. IT WAS NOT AN ILLUSION OF MY VANITY.

IN TRUTH, I CAN ONLY FAULT HIM FOR REMAINING AT NORLAND AFTER HE FIRST FELT MY INFLUENCE OVER HIM BECOMING GREATER THAN IT OUGHT TO BE. BY STAYING, HOW MUCH MORE DID HE INJURE HIMSELF? IF MY CASE IS PITIABLE, HIS IS HOPELESS.

UNLUCKY EDWARD, BOUND BY AN ENGAGEMENT THAT WAS LIKELY THE RESULT OF YOUTHFUL INFATUATION.

HOW EASILY A YOUNG MAN OF NINETEEN MIGHT SEE ONLY LUCY'S BEAUTY AND HIGH SPIRITS. BUT THE SUCCEEDING YEARS SURELY OPENED HIS EYES TO HER WANT OF EDUCATION, HER FRIVOLOUS PURSUITS, AND HER CALCULATING NATURE.

EDWARD LOVES *ME*.

I AM SURE OF IT.

AND THUS IMAGINING HIS HEART SO ALIENATED FROM LUCY, AND HOW THAT MUST PRESS UPON HIS PATIENCE...

ELINOR WEPT. FOR HIM MORE THAN FOR HERSELF.

SUPPORTED BY THE CONVICTION THAT SHE HAD DONE NOTHING TO DESERVE HER PRESENT UNHAPPINESS, AND CONSOLED BY THE BELIEF THAT EDWARD HAD DONE NOTHING TO FORFEIT HER ESTEEM, SHE THOUGHT SHE COULD EVEN NOW, UNDER THE FIRST SMART OF THE HEAVY BLOW, COMMAND HERSELF ENOUGH TO GUARD EVERY SUSPICION OF THE TRUTH FROM HER MOTHER AND SISTERS.

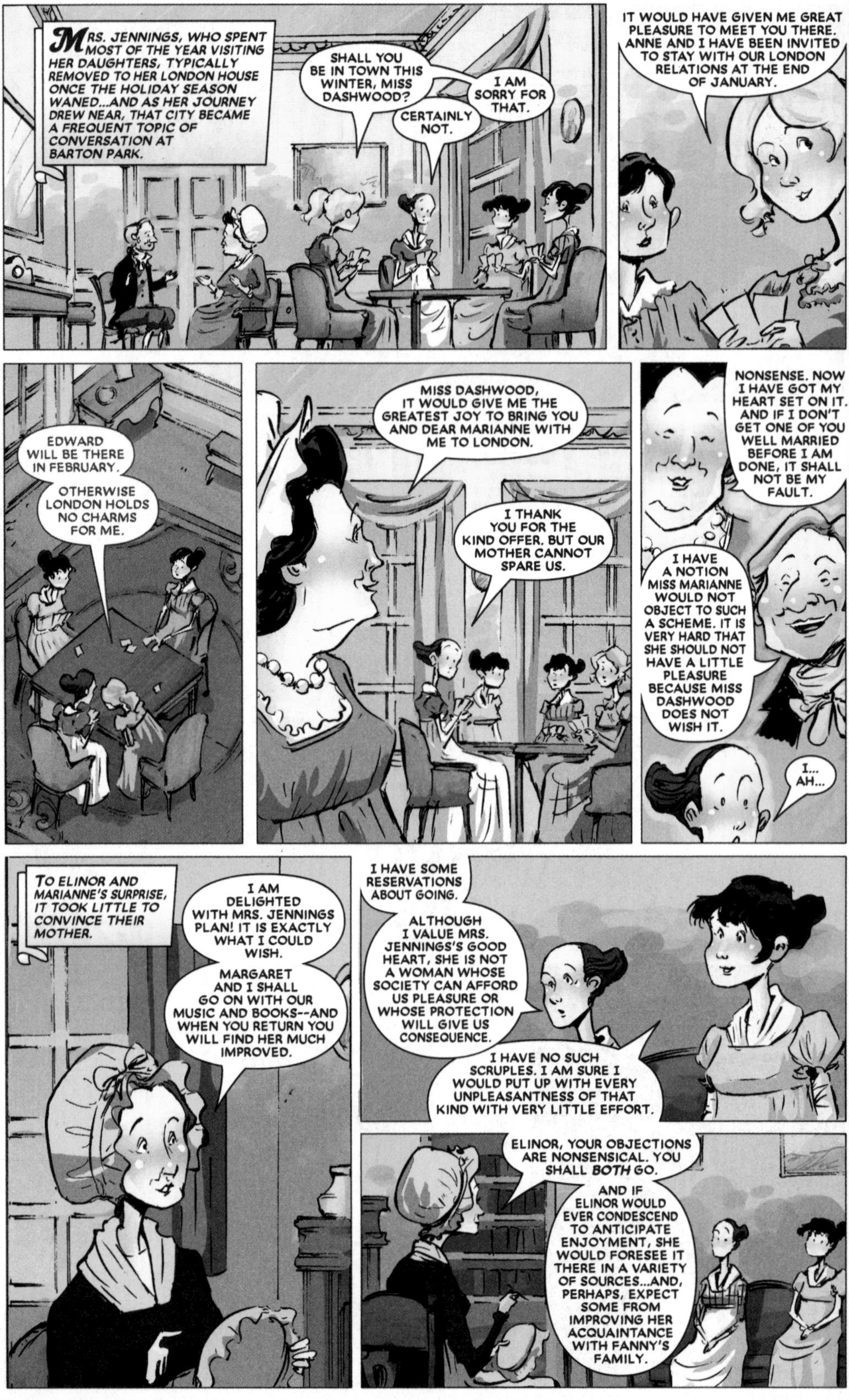

MRS. JENNINGS, WHO SPENT MOST OF THE YEAR VISITING HER DAUGHTERS, TYPICALLY REMOVED TO HER LONDON HOUSE ONCE THE HOLIDAY SEASON WANED...AND AS HER JOURNEY DREW NEAR, THAT CITY BECAME A FREQUENT TOPIC OF CONVERSATION AT BARTON PARK.
SHALL YOU BE IN TOWN THIS WINTER, MISS DASHWOOD?
CERTAINLY NOT.
I AM SORRY FOR THAT.
IT WOULD HAVE GIVEN ME GREAT PLEASURE TO MEET YOU THERE. ANNE AND I HAVE BEEN INVITED TO STAY WITH OUR LONDON RELATIONS AT THE END OF JANUARY.
EDWARD WILL BE THERE IN FEBRUARY.
OTHERWISE LONDON HOLDS NO CHARMS FOR ME.
MISS DASHWOOD, IT WOULD GIVE ME THE GREATEST JOY TO BRING YOU AND DEAR MARIANNE WITH ME TO LONDON.
I THANK YOU FOR THE KIND OFFER. BUT OUR MOTHER CANNOT SPARE US.
NONSENSE. NOW I HAVE GOT MY HEART SET ON IT. AND IF I DON'T GET ONE OF YOU WELL MARRIED BEFORE I AM DONE, IT SHALL NOT BE MY FAULT.
I HAVE A NOTION MISS MARIANNE WOULD NOT OBJECT TO SUCH A SCHEME. IT IS VERY HARD THAT SHE SHOULD NOT HAVE A LITTLE PLEASURE BECAUSE MISS DASHWOOD DOES NOT WISH IT.
I... AH...
TO ELINOR AND MARIANNE'S SURPRISE, IT TOOK LITTLE TO CONVINCE THEIR MOTHER.
I AM DELIGHTED WITH MRS. JENNINGS PLAN! IT IS EXACTLY WHAT I COULD WISH.
MARGARET AND I SHALL GO ON WITH OUR MUSIC AND BOOKS--AND WHEN YOU RETURN YOU WILL FIND HER MUCH IMPROVED.
I HAVE SOME RESERVATIONS ABOUT GOING.
ALTHOUGH I VALUE MRS. JENNINGS'S GOOD HEART, SHE IS NOT A WOMAN WHOSE SOCIETY CAN AFFORD US PLEASURE OR WHOSE PROTECTION WILL GIVE US CONSEQUENCE.
I HAVE NO SUCH SCRUPLES. I AM SURE I WOULD PUT UP WITH EVERY UNPLEASANTNESS OF THAT KIND WITH VERY LITTLE EFFORT.
ELINOR, YOUR OBJECTIONS ARE NONSENSICAL. YOU SHALL BOTH GO.
AND IF ELINOR WOULD EVER CONDESCEND TO ANTICIPATE ENJOYMENT, SHE WOULD FORESEE IT THERE IN A VARIETY OF SOURCES...AND, PERHAPS, EXPECT SOME FROM IMPROVING HER ACQUAINTANCE WITH FANNY'S FAMILY.

AND SO WITHIN THE WEEK THE DASHWOOD SISTERS FOUND THEMSELVES BUNDLED INSIDE A CHAISE WITH THEIR PATRONESS-- AND ON THEIR WAY TO LONDON.

YET FOR ALL OF MARIANNE'S EAGERNESS TO GO, SHE REMAINED WRAPT IN HER OWN MEDITATIONS DURING THE JOURNEY, AND SO ELINOR ASSIGNED HERSELF THE TASK OF OFFERING ATTENTION TO MRS. JENNINGS...

...I AM CERTAIN YOU WILL FIND LONDON TO YOUR LIKING. I WILL TAKE THE GREATEST PLEASURE IN SHOWING YOU THE TOWN.

AND MY DAUGHTER AND MR. PALMER WILL MAKE SURE YOU HAVE ANY NUMBER OF LIVELY OUTINGS TO DISTRACT YOU.

THEN I PROMISE WE WILL DO OUR BEST TO BE...DISTRACTED.

SHORTLY AFTER THEIR ARRIVAL AT MRS. JENNINGS'S HANDSOME HOUSE...

I AM WRITING HOME...HAD YOU NOT BETTER DEFER YOUR LETTER FOR A DAY OR TWO?

I AM *NOT* WRITING TO MY MOTHER.

SHE IS SURELY WRITING TO WILLOUGHBY. FOR ALL THEIR MYSTERIOUS BEHAVIOR THEY MUST BE ENGAGED.

MARIANNE SEALED UP HER NOTE AND HANDED IT TO THE FOOTMAN.

PLEASE SEE THAT THIS IS DELIVERED AT ONCE. THERE MUST BE NO DELAY.

I WILL TAKE IT MYSELF, MISS.

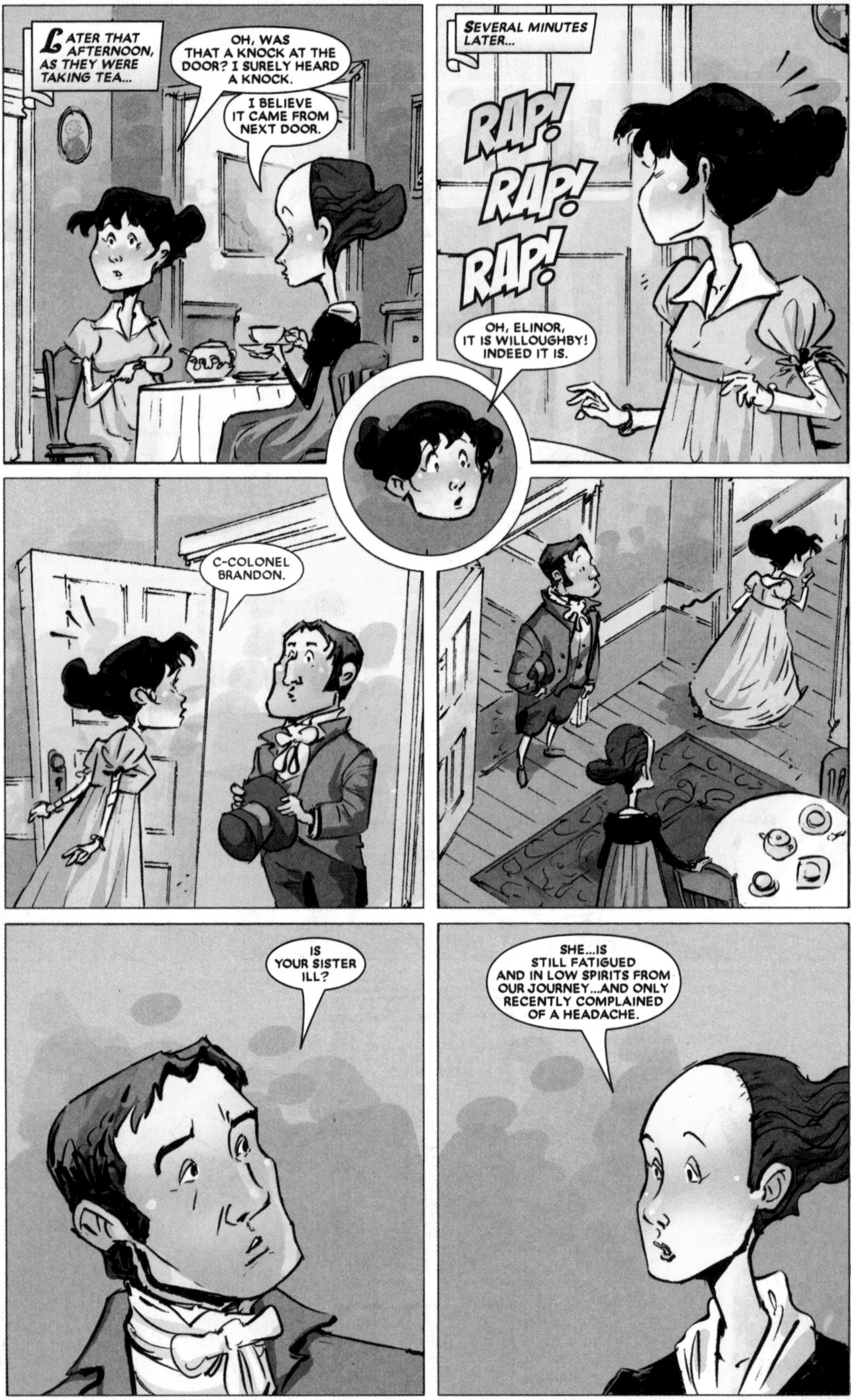
Later that afternoon, as they were taking tea...
Oh, was that a knock at the door? I surely heard a knock.
I believe it came from next door.
Several minutes later...
RAP! RAP! RAP!
Oh, Elinor, it is Willoughby! Indeed it is.
C-Colonel Brandon.
Is your sister ill?
She...is still fatigued and in low spirits from our journey...and only recently complained of a headache.

AH, COLONEL. I AM MONSTROUS GLAD TO SEE YOU. I HAVE BROUGHT TWO YOUNG LADIES WITH ME--THAT IS, YOU SEE ONE OF THEM BEFORE YOU.

THE OTHER IS ABOUT SOMEWHERE.

YOUR FRIEND MARIANNE, YOU WILL BE HAPPY TO HEAR. THOUGH WHAT YOU AND WILLOUGHBY WILL DO BETWEEN YOU ABOUT HER, I CANNOT SAY.

BUT HOW DOES YOUR BUSINESS HERE IN TOWN GO ON, COLONEL? LET US HAVE NO SECRETS AMONG FRIENDS.

THERE IS LITTLE TO TELL.

I DINED WITH THE PALMERS YESTERDAY AND CAN REPORT THAT YOUR DAUGHTER IS IN GOOD HEALTH.

THE NEXT MORNING, MARIANNE ROSE WITH RECOVERED SPIRITS-- AS THOUGH FULL OF HAPPY EXPECTATIONS FOR THE COMING DAY.

HERE IS OUR MARIANNE. MR. PALMER WILL BE SO HAPPY TO SEE YOU.

SHE MUST CERTAINLY BE A FINE SIZE BY NOW. I SHALL SEE FOR MYSELF TOMORROW, FOR SHE HAS PROMISED TO CALL ON US HERE.

WHAT DO YOU THINK HE SAID WHEN HE HEARD OF YOUR COMING WITH MAMA? I FORGET WHAT IT WAS NOW, BUT IT WAS SOMETHING SO DROLL!

NOW I AM OFF TO BOND STREET TO DO A BIT OF SHOPPING, IF YOU WOULD CARE TO JOIN ME.

MRS. JENNINGS AND ELINOR HAPPILY ASSENTED. BUT MARIANNE'S ATTENTION WAS NOT ON THE BOLTS OF DELICATE FABRIC OR THE FASHIONABLE BONNETS.

RATHER IT WAS FOCUSED ON THE STREET SCENE BEYOND THE WINDOW.

When they returned home...

HAS NO LETTER BEEN LEFT FOR ME SINCE WE WENT OUT? ARE YOU CERTAIN NO SERVANT BROUGHT A NOTE? ARE YOU QUITE SURE?

YES, MA'AM. NOTHING HAS BEEN LEFT.

HOW VERY ODD.

HOW ODD, INDEED. FOR IF SHE KNOWS WILLOUGHBY TO BE IN TOWN, HOW ODD THAT HE SHOULD NEITHER COME NOR WRITE.

I LONG TO INQUIRE, BUT HOW WILL *MY* INTERFERENCE BE BORNE?

OH, MY DEAR MOTHER, YOU MUST BE WRONG IN PERMITTING AN ENGAGEMENT BETWEEN A GIRL SO YOUNG AND A MAN SO LITTLE KNOWN.

The next morning Mrs. Jennings observed that the weather was so fine, she doubted Sir John would appreciate leaving Barton Park for London the following week.

'TIS A SAD THING FOR A SPORTSMAN TO LOSE EVEN A DAY OF PLEASURE.

THAT IS TRUE. I HAD NOT THOUGHT OF THAT. THIS WEATHER WILL KEEP MANY SPORTSMEN IN THE COUNTRY.

IT IS CHARMING WEATHER FOR THEM INDEED. THOUGH IT CANNOT LAST. FROSTS WILL SOON SET IN, IN ANOTHER DAY OR TWO. PERHAPS IT MAY FREEZE TONIGHT.

AND NOW SHE WILL WRITE TO COMBE MAGNA BY THIS DAY'S POST.

Elinor was alternately diverted and pained by Marianne, who felt in every stray breeze, and saw in every gray cloud the imminent approach of frost.

DON'T YOU FIND IT A DEAL COLDER THAN IT WAS YESTERDAY? I CAN HARDLY KEEP MY HANDS WARM.

PERHAPS A BIT COLDER.

COLONEL BRANDON BECAME A REGULAR VISITOR TO THE HOUSE, AND IT GRIEVED ELINOR TO SEE THE EARNESTNESS WITH WHICH HE REGARDED HER SISTER.

WE WERE SO HOPING TO SEE KEMBLE IN *CYMBELINE*, BUT MRS. JENNINGS SAYS TICKETS CANNOT BE GOT UNTIL EASTER AT THE EARLIEST.

WHAT?

OH, YES, I HAD HEARD THAT AS WELL.

A WEEK AFTER THEIR ARRIVAL, IT BECAME CERTAIN THAT WILLOUGHBY HAD ALSO ARRIVED IN LONDON.

GOOD GOD! HE HAS BEEN HERE WHILE WE WERE OUT!

DEPEND UPON IT--HE WILL CALL AGAIN TOMORROW.

FROM THAT MOMENT ON, MARIANNE WAS IN A STATE OF CONSTANT AGITATION, DISTRACTED BY THE EXPECTATION OF SEEING HIM EVERY HOUR OF THE DAY.

FOR ME?

NO, MA'AM, FOR MY MISTRESS.

HOW PROVOKING.

YOU ARE EXPECTING A LETTER THEN?

A LITTLE--NOT MUCH.

YOU HAVE NO CONFIDENCE IN ME, MARIANNE.

THIS REPROACH FROM *YOU*--YOU WHO CONFIDE IN NO ONE!

ME? INDEED I HAVE NOTHING TO TELL.

NOR I. OUR SITUATIONS ARE THEN ALIKE. WE NEITHER OF US HAVE ANYTHING TO TELL. YOU, BECAUSE YOU COMMUNICATE NOTHING, AND I, BECAUSE I CONCEAL NOTHING.

When the Palmers held an impromptu party of eight or nine couples, Marianne was not disposed to dance or enjoy herself in any measure.

I HAVE NEVER FELT SO FATIGUED BY DANCING.

AYE, WE KNOW THE REASON OF ALL THAT. IF A CERTAIN PERSON, WHO SHALL BE NAMELESS, HAD BEEN HERE YOU WOULD NOT HAVE BEEN A BIT TIRED.

AND TO SAY THE TRUTH, IT WAS NOT VERY PRETTY OF HIM NOT TO GIVE YOU THE MEETING WHEN HE *WAS* INVITED.

INVITED!

SO MY DAUGHTER MIDDLETON TOLD ME. IT SEEMS SIR JOHN MET HIM IN THE STREET THIS MORNING.

PLEASE DON'T FRET, MARIANNE. I'M SURE THERE IS SOME REASONABLE EXPLANATION FOR HIS ABSENCE

SIGH...

Elinor made up her mind to write to her mother—to tell her of her fears for Marianne's health. She had just finished the letter when...

COLONEL BRANDON, MA'AM.

...I'M GLAD I FIND YOU ALONE THIS MORNING, MISS DASHWOOD.

WHATEVER IS THE MATTER?

I...I WOULD LIKE TO KNOW IF I AM TO CONGRATULATE YOU ON THE ACQUISITION OF A BROTHER.

WHAT?

YOUR SISTER'S ENGAGEMENT TO WILLOUGHBY IS VERY GENERALLY KNOWN. THEIR MARRIAGE IS UNIVERSALLY TALKED OF.

IT CANNOT BE GENERALLY KNOWN, FOR HER OWN FAMILY DOES NOT KNOW OF IT.

AND BY WHOM HAVE YOU HEARD IT MENTIONED?

BY MANY...SOME WITH WHOM YOU ARE MOST INTIMATE. MRS. JENNINGS, THE PALMERS, THE MIDDLETONS.

I MIGHT NOT HAVE BELIEVED IT HAD I NOT JUST NOW SEEN A LETTER IN THE FOOTMAN'S HAND...DIRECTED TO MR. WILLOUGHBY IN YOUR SISTER'S WRITING.

I CAME TO INQUIRE, BUT WAS CONVINCED BEFORE I COULD QUESTION YOU. SO IS EVERYTHING FINALLY SETTLED? IS IT IMPOSSIBLE TO--

BUT I HAVE NO RIGHT, I COULD HAVE NO CHANCE OF SUCCEEDING. EXCUSE ME, MISS DASHWOOD, I HAVE BEEN WRONG IN SAYING SO MUCH. TELL ME ONLY THAT IT IS ALL ABSOLUTELY RESOLVED.

OH, IF I COULD BUT SHIELD HIM FROM THAT WHICH I SUSPECT.

ALTHOUGH THEY HAVE N-NEVER INFORMED ME OF THE TERMS ON WHICH THEY STAND WITH EACH OTHER, OF THEIR MUTUAL AFFECTION I HAVE NO DOUBT.

AND SO HEARING OF THEIR CORRESPONDENCE DOES NOT ASTONISH ME.

...

TO YOUR SISTER I WISH ALL IMAGINABLE HAPPINESS; TO WILLOUGHBY THAT HE MAY ENDEAVOR TO DESERVE HER.

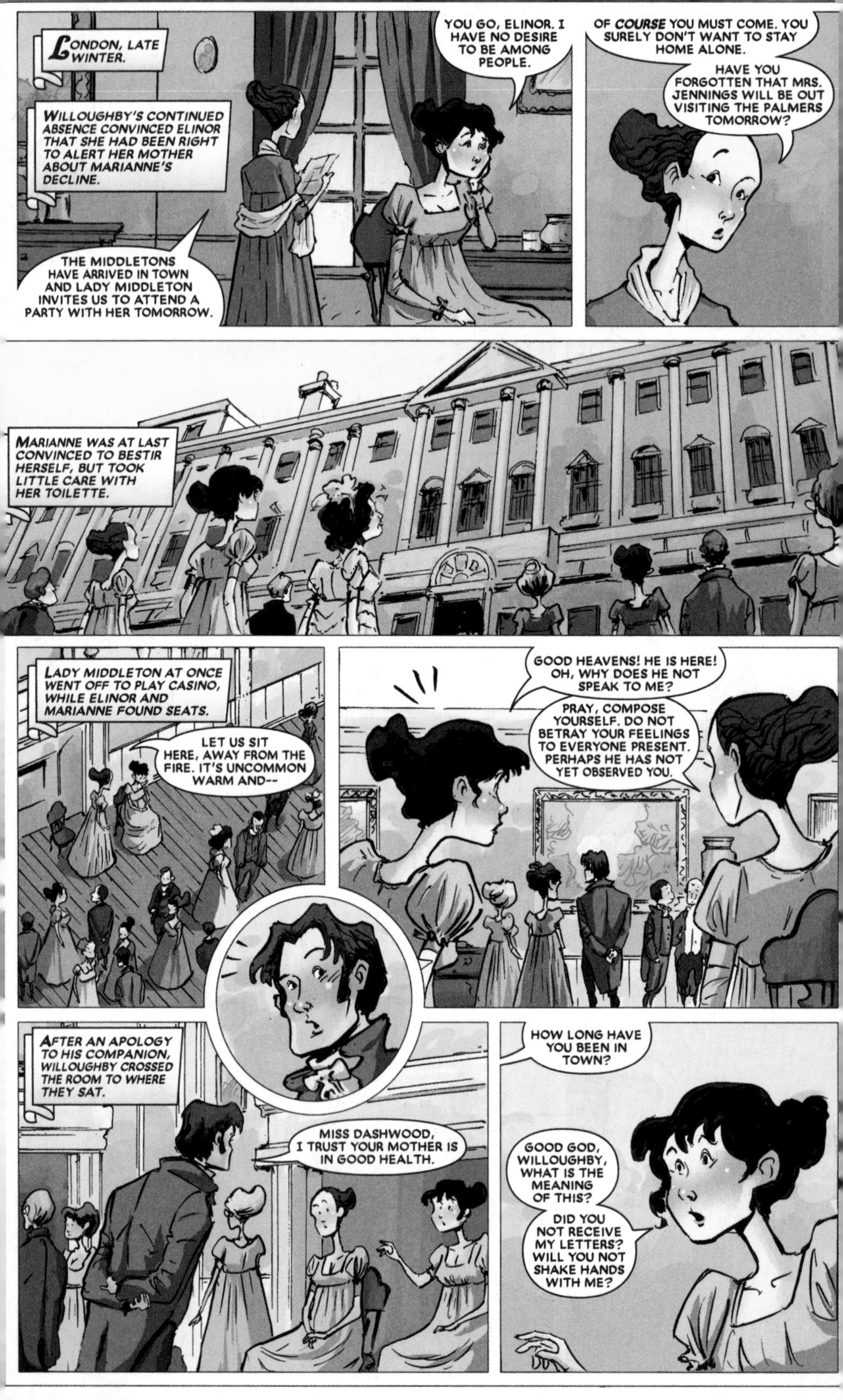
LONDON, LATE WINTER.
WILLOUGHBY'S CONTINUED ABSENCE CONVINCED ELINOR THAT SHE HAD BEEN RIGHT TO ALERT HER MOTHER ABOUT MARIANNE'S DECLINE.
THE MIDDLETONS HAVE ARRIVED IN TOWN AND LADY MIDDLETON INVITES US TO ATTEND A PARTY WITH HER TOMORROW.
YOU GO, ELINOR. I HAVE NO DESIRE TO BE AMONG PEOPLE.
OF COURSE YOU MUST COME. YOU SURELY DON'T WANT TO STAY HOME ALONE.
HAVE YOU FORGOTTEN THAT MRS. JENNINGS WILL BE OUT VISITING THE PALMERS TOMORROW?
MARIANNE WAS AT LAST CONVINCED TO BESTIR HERSELF, BUT TOOK LITTLE CARE WITH HER TOILETTE.
LADY MIDDLETON AT ONCE WENT OFF TO PLAY CASINO, WHILE ELINOR AND MARIANNE FOUND SEATS.
LET US SIT HERE, AWAY FROM THE FIRE. IT'S UNCOMMON WARM AND--
GOOD HEAVENS! HE IS HERE! OH, WHY DOES HE NOT SPEAK TO ME?
PRAY, COMPOSE YOURSELF. DO NOT BETRAY YOUR FEELINGS TO EVERYONE PRESENT. PERHAPS HE HAS NOT YET OBSERVED YOU.
AFTER AN APOLOGY TO HIS COMPANION, WILLOUGHBY CROSSED THE ROOM TO WHERE THEY SAT.
MISS DASHWOOD, I TRUST YOUR MOTHER IS IN GOOD HEALTH.
HOW LONG HAVE YOU BEEN IN TOWN?
GOOD GOD, WILLOUGHBY, WHAT IS THE MEANING OF THIS?
DID YOU NOT RECEIVE MY LETTERS? WILL YOU NOT SHAKE HANDS WITH ME?

I DID MYSELF THE HONOR OF CALLING AT BERKELEY STREET LAST TUESDAY BUT DID NOT FIND YOU OR MRS. JENNINGS AT HOME.

I HOPE MY CARD WAS NOT LOST.

BUT HAVE YOU NOT RECEIVED MY NOTES? HERE IS SOME DREADFUL MISTAKE, I AM SURE. WHAT CAN BE THE MEANING OF IT?

TELL ME, WILLOUGHBY, FOR HEAVEN'S SAKE, *TELL ME WHAT IS THE MATTER.*

... YES, I HAD THE PLEASURE OF RECEIVING THE INFORMATION OF YOUR ARRIVAL IN TOWN, WHICH YOU WERE SO GOOD TO SEND ME.

NOW, IF YOU WILL EXCUSE ME.

GO TO HIM, ELINOR, AND FORCE HIM TO COME TO ME. I MUST SPEAK TO HIM INSTANTLY. I SHALL HAVE NO PEACE UNTIL THIS IS EXPLAINED.

OH, GO THIS MOMENT.

NO, THIS IS NOT THE PLACE FOR EXPLANATIONS. WAIT ONLY UNTIL TOMORROW.

THEN I WILL GO TO HIM MYSELF.

SURELY IT WOULD SERVE YOU BETTER TO APPROACH HIM WITH SOME MEASURE OF COMPOSURE...AND IN A MORE PRIVATE PLACE.

OH, HOW SHALL I BEAR THE WAIT?

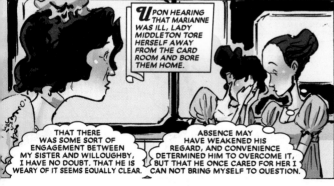

*U*PON HEARING THAT MARIANNE WAS ILL, LADY MIDDLETON TORE HERSELF AWAY FROM THE CARD ROOM AND BORE THEM HOME.

THAT THERE WAS SOME SORT OF ENGAGEMENT BETWEEN MY SISTER AND WILLOUGHBY, I HAVE NO DOUBT. THAT HE IS WEARY OF IT SEEMS EQUALLY CLEAR.

ABSENCE MAY HAVE WEAKENED HIS REGARD, AND CONVENIENCE DETERMINED HIM TO OVERCOME IT, BUT THAT HE ONCE CARED FOR HER I CAN NOT BRING MYSELF TO QUESTION.

I SHOULD FEEL THE MORE FORTUNATE, FOR I MAY CONTINUE TO ESTEEM EDWARD--EVEN THOUGH WE MIGHT BE DIVIDED-- AND SO MY MIND IS SUPPORTED.

YET EVERY CIRCUMSTANCE THAT COULD EMBITTER MARIANNE'S FINAL SEPARATION FROM WILLOUGHBY IS UNITING TO HEIGHTEN HER MISERY.

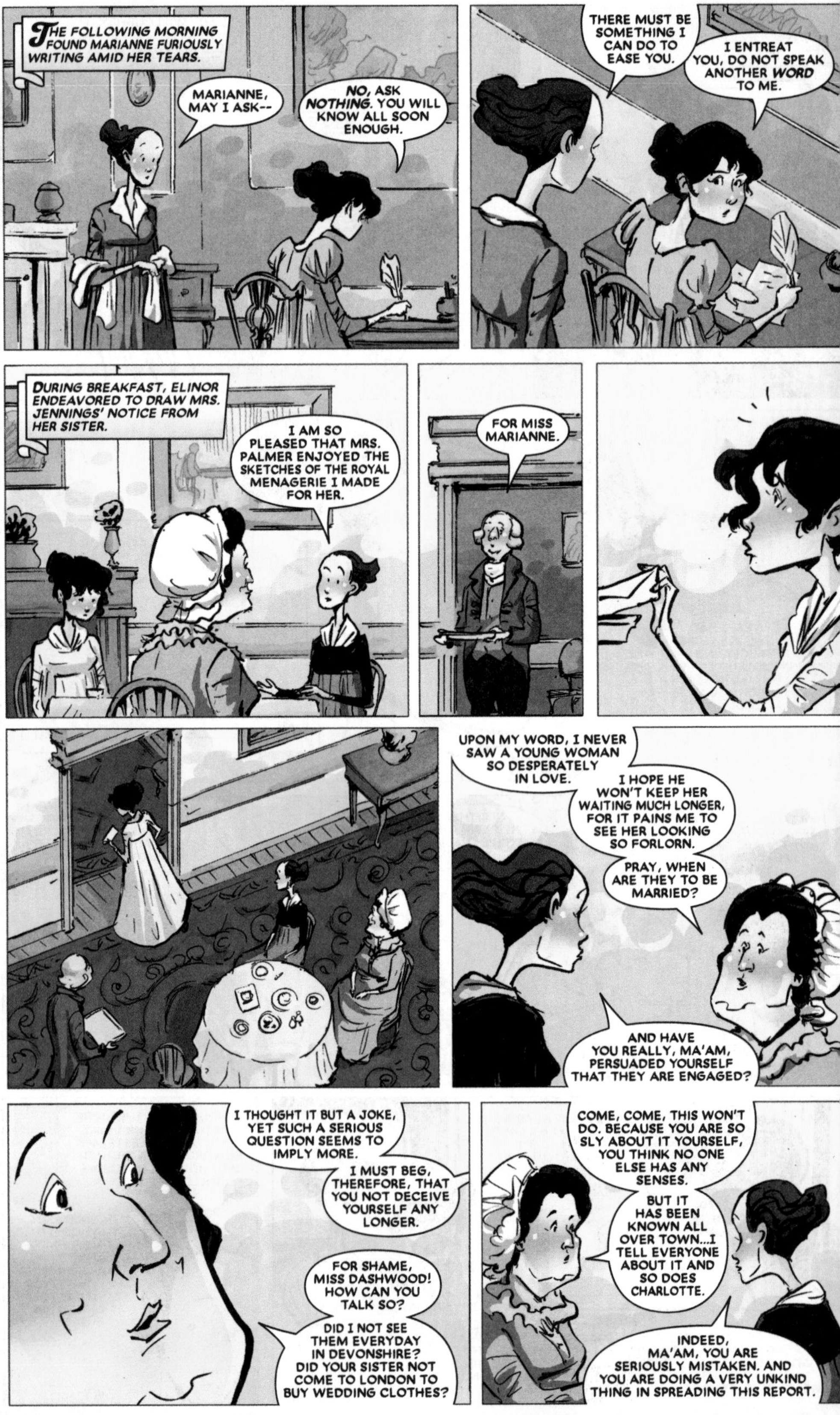
THE FOLLOWING MORNING FOUND MARIANNE FURIOUSLY WRITING AMID HER TEARS.
MARIANNE, MAY I ASK--
NO, ASK NOTHING. YOU WILL KNOW ALL SOON ENOUGH.
THERE MUST BE SOMETHING I CAN DO TO EASE YOU.
I ENTREAT YOU, DO NOT SPEAK ANOTHER WORD TO ME.
DURING BREAKFAST, ELINOR ENDEAVORED TO DRAW MRS. JENNINGS' NOTICE FROM HER SISTER.
I AM SO PLEASED THAT MRS. PALMER ENJOYED THE SKETCHES OF THE ROYAL MENAGERIE I MADE FOR HER.
FOR MISS MARIANNE.
UPON MY WORD, I NEVER SAW A YOUNG WOMAN SO DESPERATELY IN LOVE.
I HOPE HE WON'T KEEP HER WAITING MUCH LONGER, FOR IT PAINS ME TO SEE HER LOOKING SO FORLORN.
PRAY, WHEN ARE THEY TO BE MARRIED?
AND HAVE YOU REALLY, MA'AM, PERSUADED YOURSELF THAT THEY ARE ENGAGED?
I THOUGHT IT BUT A JOKE, YET SUCH A SERIOUS QUESTION SEEMS TO IMPLY MORE.
I MUST BEG, THEREFORE, THAT YOU NOT DECEIVE YOURSELF ANY LONGER.
FOR SHAME, MISS DASHWOOD! HOW CAN YOU TALK SO?
DID I NOT SEE THEM EVERYDAY IN DEVONSHIRE? DID YOUR SISTER NOT COME TO LONDON TO BUY WEDDING CLOTHES?
COME, COME, THIS WON'T DO. BECAUSE YOU ARE SO SLY ABOUT IT YOURSELF, YOU THINK NO ONE ELSE HAS ANY SENSES.
BUT IT HAS BEEN KNOWN ALL OVER TOWN...I TELL EVERYONE ABOUT IT AND SO DOES CHARLOTTE.
INDEED, MA'AM, YOU ARE SERIOUSLY MISTAKEN. AND YOU ARE DOING A VERY UNKIND THING IN SPREADING THIS REPORT.

DEAR SISTER...

READ IT...I WANT YOU TO.

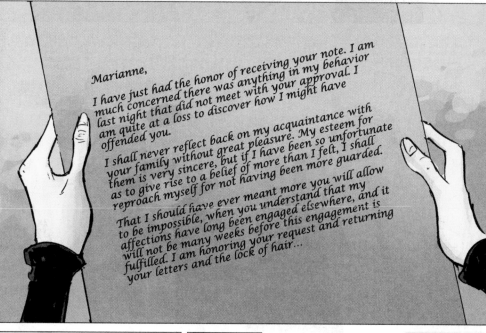

Marianne,

I have just had the honor of receiving your note. I am much concerned there was anything in my behavior last night that did not meet with your approval. I am quite at a loss to discover how I might have offended you.

I shall never reflect back on my acquaintance with your family without great pleasure. My esteem for them is very sincere, but if I have been so unfortunate as to give rise to a belief of more than I felt, I shall reproach myself for not having been more guarded.

That I should have ever meant more you will allow to be impossible, when you understand that my affections have long been engaged elsewhere, and it will not be many weeks before this engagement is fulfilled. I am honoring your request and returning your letters and the lock of hair...

AH, THIS IS IMPUDENTLY CRUEL AND WITHOUT THE LEAST DECORUM OF A GENTLEMAN.

I HAD NOT SUPPOSED HIM CAPABLE OF DEPARTING SO FAR FROM THE APPEARANCE OF EVERY DELICATE AND HONORABLE FEELING.

POOR ELINOR. HOW UNHAPPY I MAKE YOU.

I ONLY WISH THERE WERE ANYTHING I COULD DO WHICH MIGHT COMFORT YOU.

YET AS MUCH AS YOU SUFFER NOW, THINK OF YOUR SUFFERING IF THE DISCOVERY OF HIS CHARACTER HAD BEEN DELAYED, IF YOUR *ENGAGEMENT* HAD CARRIED ON FOR MONTHS AND MONTHS BEFORE HE PUT AN END TO IT.

ENGAGEMENT? THERE WAS NO ENGAGEMENT.

HE IS NOT SO UNWORTHY AS YOU BELIEVE HIM. HE BROKE NO FAITH WITH ME.

NO ENGAGEMENT? YET HE TOLD YOU HE LOVED YOU. YOU *WROTE* TO HIM.

NO...HE NEVER SAID THE WORDS. AND YES I WROTE TO HIM. COULD THAT BE WRONG AFTER ALL THAT HAD PASSED BETWEEN US?

ACH, I CANNOT TALK...

"...I HOPE THAT YOU RECEIVE THIS IN TIME TO COME HERE TO MRS. JENNINGS'S TONIGHT...I SHALL EXPECT YOU HERE TOMORROW...I CANNOT EXPRESS MY ASTONISHMENT AT NOT HAVING RECEIVED AN ANSWER TO MY NOTE...I HAVE BEEN EXPECTING TO SEE YOU EVERY HOUR OF THE DAY...

"WHAT AM I TO IMAGINE, WILLOUGHBY, BY YOUR BEHAVIOR OF LAST NIGHT?"

I FELT MYSELF TO BE AS SOLEMNLY ENGAGED TO HIM AS IF BOUND BY THE STRICTEST LEGAL COVENANT.

I CAN BELIEVE IT. BUT SADLY, HE DID NOT FEEL THE SAME.

I WANT TO GO HOME...I MUST GO AND COMFORT MAMA, WHO WILL FEEL HIS LOSS NEARLY AS GREATLY AS I DO.

I...I WANT TO LEAVE TOMORROW, BEFORE ALL THE PITYING STARES AND CRUEL REMARKS BEGIN.

IT WOULD BE IMPOSSIBLE TO LEAVE SO SOON. WE OWE MRS. JENNINGS MUCH MORE THAN CIVILITY, BUT CIVILITY ALONE MUST PREVENT SUCH A HASTY REMOVAL.

BUT I ONLY CAME FOR WILLOUGHBY'S SAKE. NOW WHO CARES FOR ME OR REGARDS ME?

I DO. NOW LIE BACK AND I WILL DAB SOME LAVENDER DROPS ON YOUR BROW.

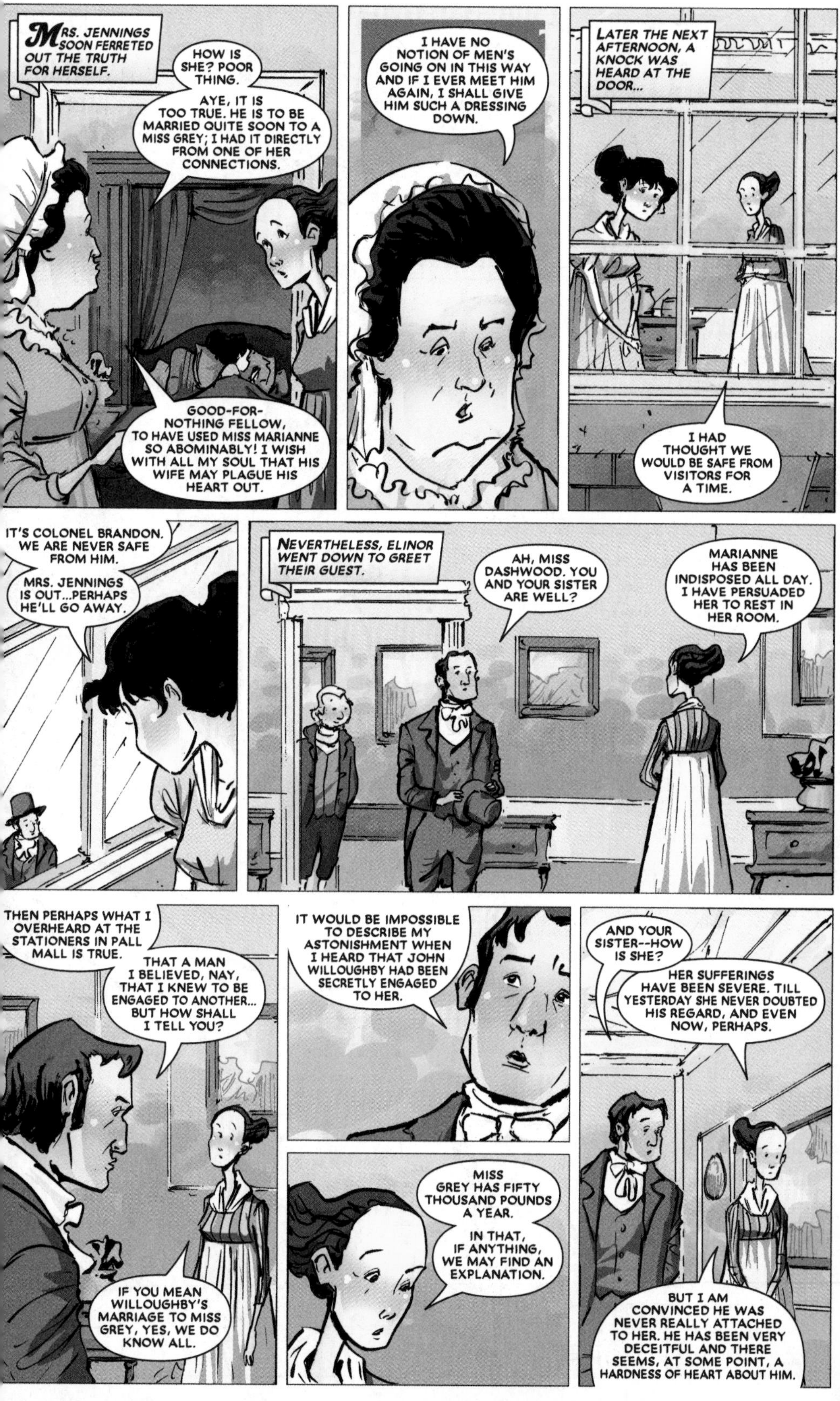
MRS. JENNINGS SOON FERRETED OUT THE TRUTH FOR HERSELF.
HOW IS SHE? POOR THING.
AYE, IT IS TOO TRUE. HE IS TO BE MARRIED QUITE SOON TO A MISS GREY; I HAD IT DIRECTLY FROM ONE OF HER CONNECTIONS.
GOOD-FOR-NOTHING FELLOW, TO HAVE USED MISS MARIANNE SO ABOMINABLY! I WISH WITH ALL MY SOUL THAT HIS WIFE MAY PLAGUE HIS HEART OUT.
I HAVE NO NOTION OF MEN'S GOING ON IN THIS WAY AND IF I EVER MEET HIM AGAIN, I SHALL GIVE HIM SUCH A DRESSING DOWN.
LATER THE NEXT AFTERNOON, A KNOCK WAS HEARD AT THE DOOR...
I HAD THOUGHT WE WOULD BE SAFE FROM VISITORS FOR A TIME.
IT'S COLONEL BRANDON. WE ARE NEVER SAFE FROM HIM.
MRS. JENNINGS IS OUT...PERHAPS HE'LL GO AWAY.
NEVERTHELESS, ELINOR WENT DOWN TO GREET THEIR GUEST.
AH, MISS DASHWOOD. YOU AND YOUR SISTER ARE WELL?
MARIANNE HAS BEEN INDISPOSED ALL DAY. I HAVE PERSUADED HER TO REST IN HER ROOM.
THEN PERHAPS WHAT I OVERHEARD AT THE STATIONERS IN PALL MALL IS TRUE.
THAT A MAN I BELIEVED, NAY, THAT I KNEW TO BE ENGAGED TO ANOTHER... BUT HOW SHALL I TELL YOU?
IF YOU MEAN WILLOUGHBY'S MARRIAGE TO MISS GREY, YES, WE DO KNOW ALL.
IT WOULD BE IMPOSSIBLE TO DESCRIBE MY ASTONISHMENT WHEN I HEARD THAT JOHN WILLOUGHBY HAD BEEN SECRETLY ENGAGED TO HER.
MISS GREY HAS FIFTY THOUSAND POUNDS A YEAR.
IN THAT, IF ANYTHING, WE MAY FIND AN EXPLANATION.
AND YOUR SISTER--HOW IS SHE?
HER SUFFERINGS HAVE BEEN SEVERE. TILL YESTERDAY SHE NEVER DOUBTED HIS REGARD, AND EVEN NOW, PERHAPS.
BUT I AM CONVINCED HE WAS NEVER REALLY ATTACHED TO HER. HE HAS BEEN VERY DECEITFUL AND THERE SEEMS, AT SOME POINT, A HARDNESS OF HEART ABOUT HIM.

I MIGHT HAVE THE MEANS OF GIVING HER... COMFORT.

NO, I MUST NOT SAY COMFORT, BUT A CONVICTION, A LASTING CONVICTION IN YOUR SISTER'S MIND.

MY GRATITUDE FOR SUCH INFORMATION WILL BE IMMEDIATE, EVEN IF HERS MUST BE GAINED BY IT IN TIME.

DO I UNDERSTAND YOU HAVE SOMETHING TO TELL ME OF WILLOUGHBY THAT WILL OPEN HIS CHARACTER FURTHER?

IF SO, YOUR TELLING IT WOULD BE THE GREATEST ACT OF FRIENDSHIP THAT CAN BE SHOWN MARIANNE.

YOU MAY RECALL A CONVERSATION WE HAD AT BARTON PARK IN WHICH I ALLUDED TO A LADY I HAD ONCE KNOWN.

YOU SAID MY SISTER REMINDED YOU OF HER IN SOME MEASURE.

THERE IS A STRONG RESEMBLANCE-- THE SAME WARMTH OF HEART, THE SAME EAGERNESS OF FANCY AND SPIRITS.

THIS LADY WAS ONE OF MY NEAREST RELATIONS, AN ORPHAN FROM INFANCY AND UNDER MY FATHER'S GUARDIANSHIP. WE WERE PLAYFELLOWS AS CHILDREN AND...

I CANNOT RECALL WHEN I DID NOT LOVE ELIZA. HER AFFECTION FOR ME WAS AS FERVENT AS YOUR SISTER'S FOR WILLOUGHBY.

AT SEVENTEEN SHE WAS LOST TO ME, MARRIED AGAINST HER INCLINATION TO MY OLDER BROTHER. HER FORTUNE WAS LARGE AND MY FAMILY MUCH ENCUMBERED. MY BROTHER DID NOT DESERVE HER, HE DID NOT LOVE HER.

AH, I AM AN AWKWARD NARRATOR...WE'D PLANNED TO ELOPE, YOU SEE, BUT WERE BETRAYED.

I WAS BANISHED FROM MY FATHER'S HOUSE, AND THE WEDDING WENT FORWARD AS PLANNED.

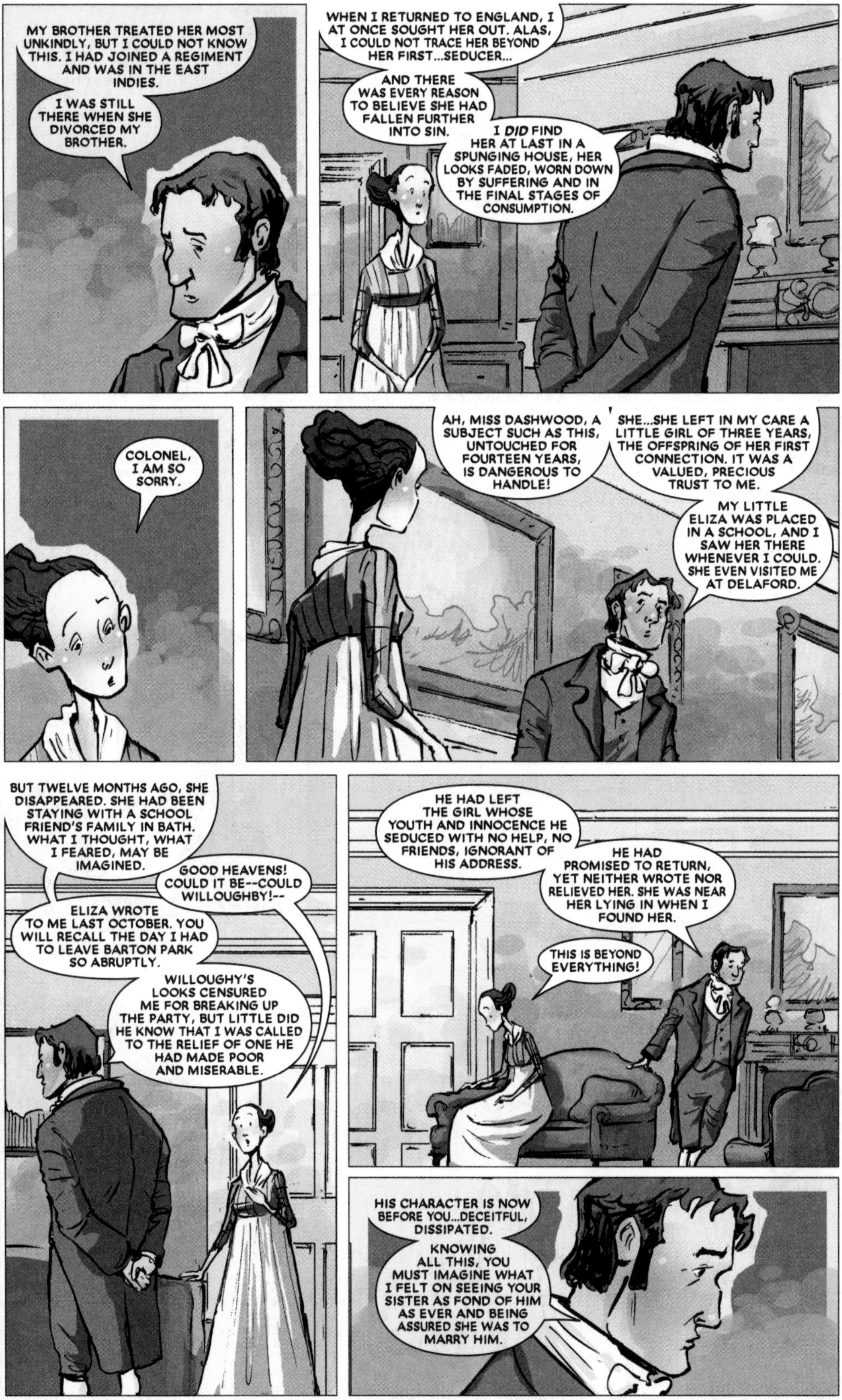
MY BROTHER TREATED HER MOST UNKINDLY, BUT I COULD NOT KNOW THIS. I HAD JOINED A REGIMENT AND WAS IN THE EAST INDIES.
I WAS STILL THERE WHEN SHE DIVORCED MY BROTHER.
WHEN I RETURNED TO ENGLAND, I AT ONCE SOUGHT HER OUT. ALAS, I COULD NOT TRACE HER BEYOND HER FIRST...SEDUCER...
AND THERE WAS EVERY REASON TO BELIEVE SHE HAD FALLEN FURTHER INTO SIN.
I *DID* FIND HER AT LAST IN A SPUNGING HOUSE, HER LOOKS FADED, WORN DOWN BY SUFFERING AND IN THE FINAL STAGES OF CONSUMPTION.
COLONEL, I AM SO SORRY.
AH, MISS DASHWOOD, A SUBJECT SUCH AS THIS, UNTOUCHED FOR FOURTEEN YEARS, IS DANGEROUS TO HANDLE!
SHE...SHE LEFT IN MY CARE A LITTLE GIRL OF THREE YEARS, THE OFFSPRING OF HER FIRST CONNECTION. IT WAS A VALUED, PRECIOUS TRUST TO ME.
MY LITTLE ELIZA WAS PLACED IN A SCHOOL, AND I SAW HER THERE WHENEVER I COULD. SHE EVEN VISITED ME AT DELAFORD.
BUT TWELVE MONTHS AGO, SHE DISAPPEARED. SHE HAD BEEN STAYING WITH A SCHOOL FRIEND'S FAMILY IN BATH. WHAT I THOUGHT, WHAT I FEARED, MAY BE IMAGINED.
GOOD HEAVENS! COULD IT BE--COULD WILLOUGHBY!--
ELIZA WROTE TO ME LAST OCTOBER. YOU WILL RECALL THE DAY I HAD TO LEAVE BARTON PARK SO ABRUPTLY.
WILLOUGHY'S LOOKS CENSURED ME FOR BREAKING UP THE PARTY, BUT LITTLE DID HE KNOW THAT I WAS CALLED TO THE RELIEF OF ONE HE HAD MADE POOR AND MISERABLE.
HE HAD LEFT THE GIRL WHOSE YOUTH AND INNOCENCE HE SEDUCED WITH NO HELP, NO FRIENDS, IGNORANT OF HIS ADDRESS.
HE HAD PROMISED TO RETURN, YET NEITHER WROTE NOR RELIEVED HER. SHE WAS NEAR HER LYING IN WHEN I FOUND HER.
THIS IS BEYOND EVERYTHING!
HIS CHARACTER IS NOW BEFORE YOU...DECEITFUL, DISSIPATED.
KNOWING ALL THIS, YOU MUST IMAGINE WHAT I FELT ON SEEING YOUR SISTER AS FOND OF HIM AS EVER AND BEING ASSURED SHE WAS TO MARRY HIM.

USE YOUR OWN DISCRETION IN COMMUNICATING TO HER WHAT I HAVE TOLD YOU.

WHATEVER WILLOUGHBY'S INTENTIONS WERE TOWARD YOUR SISTER, SHE WILL SOON TURN WITH GRATITUDE TOWARD HER OWN CONDITION WHEN SHE COMPARES IT TO THAT OF MY POOR ELIZA.

I HAVE BEEN MORE PAINED BY HER ENDEAVORS TO ACQUIT HIM THAN ALL THE REST. NOW I AM SURE SHE WILL BECOME EASIER IN HER MIND.

HAVE...HAVE YOU SEEN MR. WILLOUGHBY SINCE YOU LEFT BARTON PARK?

ONE MEETING WAS INEVITABLE.

WHAT! HAVE YOU MET HIM TO--

I COULD MEET HIM NO OTHER WAY. WE MET BY APPOINTMENT, HE TO DEFEND, I TO PUNISH HIS CONDUCT. WE RETURNED UNWOUNDED AND SO NEWS OF THE MEETING NEVER GOT ABROAD.

ELIZA AND HER CHILD HAVE BEEN SENT TO THE COUNTRY. SUCH HAS BEEN THE UNHAPPY RESEMBLANCE BETWEEN MOTHER AND DAUGHTER! AND SO IMPERFECTLY HAVE I DISCHARGED MY TRUST.

AFTER COLONEL BRANDON'S DEPARTURE, ELINOR WENT AT ONCE TO MARIANNE AND RELAYED HIS TALE.

...OH, THE MISERY OF THAT POOR, POOR GIRL. I WEEP IN COMPASSION FOR HER AND FOR COLONEL BRANDON...

PERHAPS YOUR SPIRITS WILL BE LESS AGITATED NOW, DEAREST. I WILL LEAVE YOU TO SLEEP A LITTLE BEFORE SUPPER.

BUT, OH, ELINOR, I WEEP FOR MYSELF AS WELL. I FEEL THE LOSS OF WILLOUGHBY'S CHARACTER FAR MORE ACUTELY THAN THE LOSS OF HIS HEART.

IF ELINOR THOUGHT BRANDON'S REVELATION WOULD MAKE MARIANNE LESS WRETCHED, SHE WAS MISTAKEN.

HER SISTER SUCCUMBED TO A BROODING SORROW--ESPECIALLY WHEN NEWS REACHED HER THAT WILLOUGHBY'S WEDDING HAD TAKEN PLACE.

I advise you to remain in London. It would be better for Marianne to be anywhere than at Barton, where everything within her view would bring back the past in the strongest and most afflicting manner.

MAMA WRITES THAT JOHN AND FANNY WILL BE IN TOWN SHORTLY. SHE JUDGES THAT IT WOULD BE RIGHT FOR US TO SOMETIMES VISIT OUR BROTHER.

YOU NEEDN'T WORRY THAT YOU WILL SEE *HIM* IF WE GO OUT AMONG OUR FRIENDS... HE LEFT TOWN DIRECTLY AFTER THE WEDDING.

I WILL DO WHATEVER MAMA WISHES.

ELINOR'S ONE CONSOLATION WAS THAT MARIANNE NOW WELCOMED COLONEL BRANDON'S VISITS AND OFTEN SAT CONVERSING WITH HIM IN THE GENTLEST TONES.

IS THAT WHERE YOU WERE STATIONED, COLONEL? IN KASHMIR?

YES, AT THE FOOT OF THE HIMALAYAS.

EVEN YOU, WHO HAVE A GREAT AFFINITY FOR THE PICTURESQUE, WOULD FIND YOURSELF AT A LOSS FOR WORDS WERE YOU CALLED UPON TO DESCRIBE THOSE PEAKS.

I WOULD CALL THEM PEERLESS...AND PROFOUND.

AT THE END OF FEBRUARY, LUCY AND ANNE STEELE ARRIVED AT THEIR COUSIN'S HOUSE AND IMMEDIATELY CALLED AT BERKELEY STREET.

IMAGINE MY DELIGHT IN FINDING YOU *STILL* IN TOWN, MISS DASHWOOD.

I KNOW YOU *TOLD* ME YOU SHOULD NOT STAY ABOVE A MONTH.

BUT IT WOULD HAVE BEEN A PITY TO LEAVE BEFORE YOUR BROTHER AND SISTER CAME.

I AM *SURE* YOU WILL NOW BE IN NO HURRY TO BE GONE.

I AM AMAZINGLY GLAD YOU DID NOT KEEP *YOUR WORD.*

I EXPECT YOU WILL GO AND STAY WITH YOUR BROTHER WHEN HE COMES TO TOWN.

NO, I DO NOT THINK WE SHALL.

OH, YES, I DARESAY YOU WILL.

I AM SORRY TO HEAR YOUR SISTER IS INDISPOSED. I THINK SHE MIGHT SEE *US.*

AND I AM SURE WE WOULD NOT SPEAK A *WORD.*

SHE IS ABED OR IN HER DRESSING GOWN.

OH, IF THAT'S ALL, THEN WE CAN GO AND SEE *HER.*

DON'T BE FORWARD, ANNE. MISS DASHWOOD WILL THINK US ILL BRED.

SEVERAL MORNINGS LATER, THE DASHWOOD SISTERS WERE ENGAGED IN A COMMISSION FOR THEIR MOTHER--SELLING SEVERAL OF HER JEWELS.

YES, I AM INTERESTED IN SELECTING A TOOTHPICK CASE.

AH, THIS ENGRAVED ONE IS VERY NICE...

BUT THIS GEM...IS THAT A REAL PEARL? ONE CAN'T BE TOO CAREFUL.

THEN AGAIN, THIS IVORY ONE IS QUITE ELEGANT...OR PERHAPS THIS ONE SHAPED LIKE AN URN.

WHATEVER YOU WISH, MR. FERRARS.

COULD THAT BE *ROBERT* FERRARS?

HOW ODD THAT EDWARD SHOULD HAVE SUCH A COXCOMB FOR A BROTHER.

ONCE THE GENTLEMAN HAD SAUNTERED OFF, ELINOR APPROACHED THE COUNTER.

JOHN!

ELINOR, GOOD HEAVENS! AND MARIANNE AS WELL. I WAS GOING TO CALL ON YOU YESTERDAY BUT WE WERE OBLIGED TO VISIT MRS. FERRARS.

YOUNG HARRY WAS VASTLY PLEASED. WHAT SAY I COME HOME WITH YOU NOW AND MEET MRS. JENNINGS? I UNDERSTAND SHE IS A LADY OF VERY GOOD FORTUNE.

SHE WILL BE WAITING OUTSIDE FOR US WITH HER CARRIAGE. SHE HAS BEEN MOST KIND TO US, AS HAVE HER DAUGHTER AND SON-IN-LAW.

THEIR ATTENTION TO OUR COMFORT IS MORE THAN I CAN EXPRESS.

I AM EXTREMELY GLAD TO HEAR OF IT.

SO YOU ARE MOST COMFORTABLY SETTLED IN YOUR COTTAGE AND WANT FOR NOTHING! EDWARD BROUGHT US A MOST CHARMING ACCOUNT OF THE PLACE. IT WAS A GREAT SATISFACTION TO HEAR IT.

ELINOR'S SHARP RETORT WAS CUT OFF BY MRS. JENNINGS HERSELF.

COME, COME, GIRLS. WHAT'S THE DELAY?

MRS. JENNINGS, LET ME MAKE KNOWN TO YOU MY BROTHER, JOHN DASHWOOD.

MR. DASHWOOD, YOU MUST COME TO TEA THIS VERY INSTANT. I INSIST ON IT.

JOHN DULY PAID HIS CALL, THEN ASKED ELINOR TO WALK WITH HIM TO CONDUIT STREET AND INTRODUCE HIM TO THE MIDDLETONS.

AS THEY WERE LEAVING, THEY PASSED COLONEL BRANDON IN THE HALL, ON HIS WAY TO VISIT MARIANNE.

WHO IS THIS COLONEL BRANDON? A MAN OF FORTUNE?

YES, HE HAS A VERY GOOD PROPERTY IN DORSETSHIRE.

I AM GLAD OF IT. HE SEEMED MOST GENTLEMAN-LIKE.

I THINK I MIGHT CONGRATULATE YOU, ELINOR, ON THE PROSPECT OF A VERY RESPECTABLE ESTABLISHMENT IN LIFE.

ME, BROTHER? WHAT DO YOU MEAN? HE HAS NO WISH TO MARRY *ME*!

HE LIKES YOU. I OBSERVED HIM NARROWLY AND AM CONVINCED OF IT. A LITTLE TROUBLE ON YOUR SIDE SECURES HIM.

IT WOULD BE SOMETHING DROLL IF FANNY AND I EACH HAD A SIBLING SETTLING AT THE SAME TIME.

IS EDWARD FERRARS GOING TO BE MARRIED?

NOTHING IS ACTUALLY ARRANGED.

THE LADY IS THE HON. MISS MORTON WITH THIRTY THOUSAND POUNDS. A VERY DESIRABLE CONNECTION ON BOTH SIDES. MRS. FERRARS WILL SETTLE A THOUSAND POUNDS A YEAR ON HIM IF THE MATCH TAKES PLACE.

THAT IS A GREAT DEAL FOR A MOTHER TO GIVE AWAY. BUT MRS. FERRARS HAS A NOBLE SPIRIT.

WHY, JUST THE OTHER DAY, AWARE THAT MONEY WAS NOT PLENTIFUL WITH US, SHE PUT BANK NOTES AMOUNTING TO TWO HUNDRED POUNDS INTO FANNY'S HANDS.

YOUR EXPENSES IN TOWN AND COUNTRY MUST BE CONSIDERABLE, YET YOUR INCOME IS LARGE.

NOT SO LARGE AS MANY SUPPOSE. TAKE, FOR INSTANCE, THE INEVITABLE EXPENSE WE BORE ON FIRST COMING TO NORLAND.

OUR FATHER BEQUEATHED ALL HIS EFFECTS--AND VERY VALUABLE THEY WERE--TO YOUR MOTHER.

OF COURSE HE HAD A RIGHT TO DISPOSE OF HIS PROPERTY AS HE CHOSE, BUT WE HAVE HAD TO REPLACE ALL THE LINEN AND CHINA THAT WAS TAKEN AWAY.

YOU MAY GUESS, AFTER ALL THESE EXPENSES, HOW VERY FAR WE MUST BE FROM BEING RICH, AND HOW WELCOME MRS. FERRARS'S KINDESS IS.

ASSISTED BY HER LIBERALITY, I HOPE YOU MAY YET LIVE TO BE IN EASY CIRCUMSTANCES.

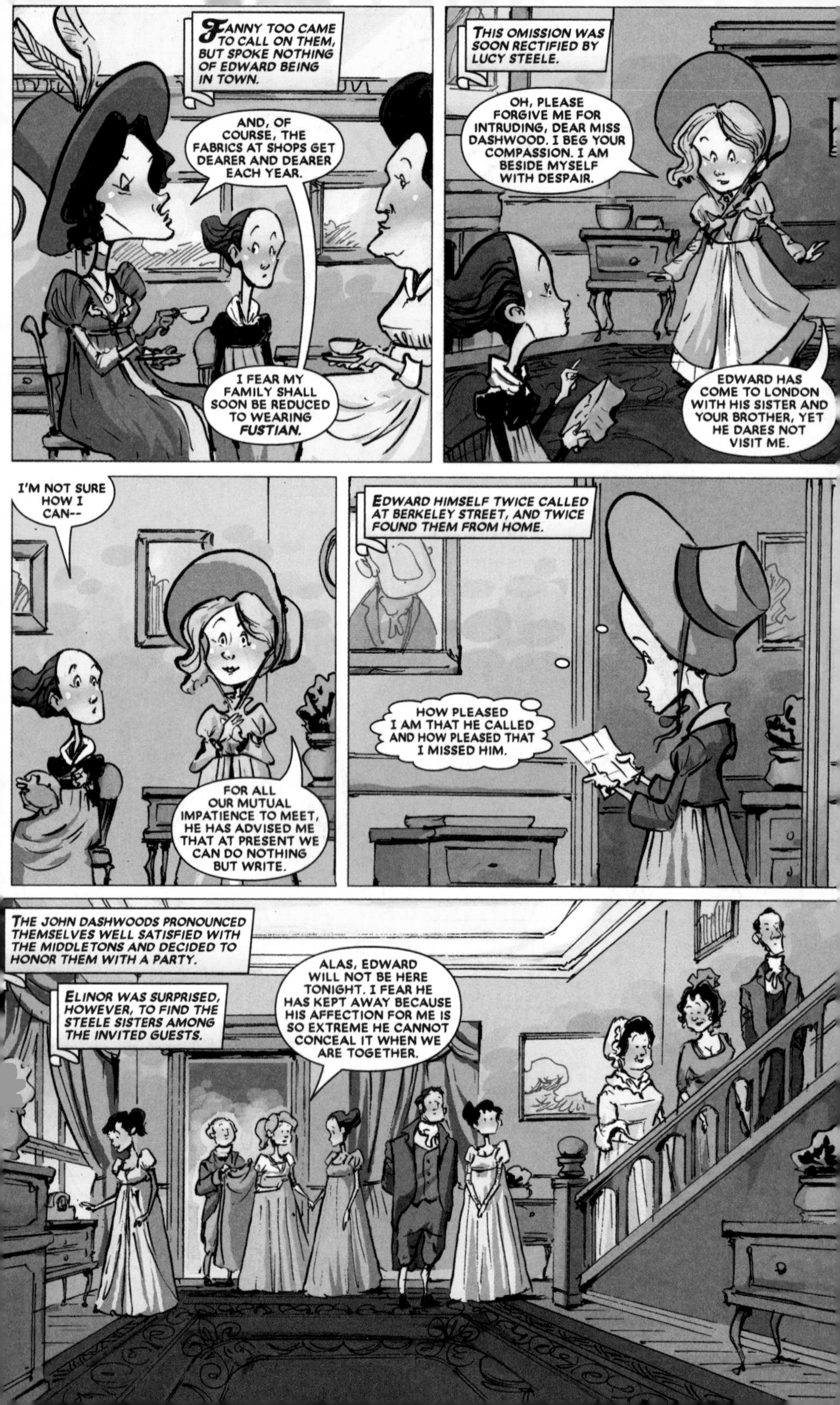
FANNY TOO CAME TO CALL ON THEM, BUT SPOKE NOTHING OF EDWARD BEING IN TOWN.
AND, OF COURSE, THE FABRICS AT SHOPS GET DEARER AND DEARER EACH YEAR.
I FEAR MY FAMILY SHALL SOON BE REDUCED TO WEARING FUSTIAN.
THIS OMISSION WAS SOON RECTIFIED BY LUCY STEELE.
OH, PLEASE FORGIVE ME FOR INTRUDING, DEAR MISS DASHWOOD. I BEG YOUR COMPASSION. I AM BESIDE MYSELF WITH DESPAIR.
EDWARD HAS COME TO LONDON WITH HIS SISTER AND YOUR BROTHER, YET HE DARES NOT VISIT ME.
I'M NOT SURE HOW I CAN--
FOR ALL OUR MUTUAL IMPATIENCE TO MEET, HE HAS ADVISED ME THAT AT PRESENT WE CAN DO NOTHING BUT WRITE.
EDWARD HIMSELF TWICE CALLED AT BERKELEY STREET, AND TWICE FOUND THEM FROM HOME.
HOW PLEASED I AM THAT HE CALLED AND HOW PLEASED THAT I MISSED HIM.
THE JOHN DASHWOODS PRONOUNCED THEMSELVES WELL SATISFIED WITH THE MIDDLETONS AND DECIDED TO HONOR THEM WITH A PARTY.
ELINOR WAS SURPRISED, HOWEVER, TO FIND THE STEELE SISTERS AMONG THE INVITED GUESTS.
ALAS, EDWARD WILL NOT BE HERE TONIGHT. I FEAR HE HAS KEPT AWAY BECAUSE HIS AFFECTION FOR ME IS SO EXTREME HE CANNOT CONCEAL IT WHEN WE ARE TOGETHER.

PITY ME, MISS DASHWOOD. THERE IS NOBODY HERE BUT YOU THAT CAN FEEL FOR ME.

IN A MOMENT I SHALL MEET THE PERSON THAT ALL MY HAPPINESS DEPENDS ON--THAT IS TO BE MY MOTHER.

OR MORE LIKELY TO BE MISS MORTON'S *NEW* MOTHER, IF LUCY ONLY KNEW IT.

INDEED, I DO PITY YOU, LUCY.

Elinor was presented to Mrs. Ferrars, whom she found stiff and ill-natured.

MISS DASHWOOD, I BELIEVE YOU AND YOUR FAMILY ARE...*TENANTS* ON SIR JOHN'S PROPERTY IN DEVON.

SIR JOHN MIDDLETON IS MY MOTHER'S COUSIN, MA'AM.

The Misses Steele, however, were welcomed graciously by both mother and daughter.

HOW I LONG TO MEET YOUR GRANDSON, MRS. FERRARS. ANNE AND I BOTH ADORE YOUNG CHILDREN.

After dinner, the group made their way to the drawing room.

MISS DASHWOOD MADE THESE FOR ME WHILE WE WERE TOGETHER AT NORLAND.

HUM...VERY PRETTY.

DO YOU NOT THINK THEM IN MISS MORTON'S STYLE OF PAINTING? SHE *DOES* PAINT MOST DELIGHTFULLY.

HOW BEAUTIFUL HER LAST LANDSCAPE IS DONE.

BEAUTIFULLY INDEED! BUT THEN *SHE* DOES EVERYTHING WELL.

THIS IS PRAISE OF A VERY PARTICULAR KIND. WHO IS MISS MORTON? WHO KNOWS OR CARES FOR HER?

IT IS ELINOR OF WHOM *WE* THINK AND SPEAK.

MARIANNE!

MISS MORTON IS *LORD* MORTON'S DAUGHTER.

HOW THEY GLARE AT HER, YET I SEE ONLY AN AFFECTIONATE CREATURE WHO CANNOT BEAR TO HEAR HER SISTER SLIGHTED.

DEAR ELINOR, DON'T MIND THEM. DON'T LET THEM MAKE *YOU* UNHAPPY.

POOR MARIANNE. SHE HAS NOT SUCH GOOD HEALTH AS HER SISTER.

IT MUST BE VERY TRYING FOR ONE WHO *HAS BEEN* A BEAUTY TO HAVE LOST HER PERSONAL ATTRACTION.

*T*HE NEXT MORNING, ELINOR ASSESSED HER MEETING WITH MRS. FERRARS.

I BELIEVE I SAW ENOUGH OF HER PRIDE, HER MEANNESS, HER DETERMINED PREJUDICE AGAINST ME...TO COMPREHEND ALL THE DIFFICULTIES THAT MIGHT HAVE PERPLEXED MY ENGAGEMENT TO EDWARD, HAD HE BEEN FREE.

AND I AM FURTHER CONVINCED THAT MRS. FERRARS'S PREFERENCE FOR LUCY--THOUGH I AM SURE MISS STEELE'S VANITY MADE HER BLIND TO IT--WAS SIMPLY BECAUSE SHE WAS NOT *ME*.

*L*UCY HERSELF ARRIVED NOT TEN MINUTES LATER...TO GLOAT.

MY DEAR FRIEND, I AM SO HAPPY. COULD MRS. FERRARS'S BEHAVIOR TOWARD ME BE ANY MORE FLATTERING? THERE WAS SUCH AFFABILITY IN HER MANNER...I WAS SURE SHE HAD QUITE TOOK A FANCY TO ME.

YOU SHAN'T TALK ME OUT OF MY SATISFACTION. MRS. FERRARS IS A CHARMING WOMAN, AND SO IS YOUR SISTER. BOTH DELIGHTFUL WOMEN, INDEED!

I WONDER I NEVER HEAR YOU SAY HOW AGREEABLE MRS. DASHWOOD IS.

ARE YOU ILL, MISS DASHWOOD? YOU SEEM LOW...YOU DON'T SPEAK.

I WAS NEVER IN BETTER HEALTH.

SHE WAS CERTAINLY VERY CIVIL TO YOU. IF THEY HAD KNOWN OF YOUR ENGAGEMENT, NOTHING COULD BE MORE FLATTERING THAN THEIR TREATMENT OF YOU. BUT AS THAT WAS NOT THE CASE--

MR. FERRARS.

MISS DASHWOOD...I AM SO PLEASED THAT YOU ARE--

EDWARD, I AM SO PLEASED TO SEE YOU.

I BELIEVE YOU KNOW *MISS STEELE*...FROM PLYMOUTH.

ER...YES, OF COURSE. MISS STEELE, I GIVE YOU GOOD DAY.

EDWARD, YOU MUST LET ME FETCH MARIANNE DOWN FROM HER ROOM. SHE WILL BE SO HAPPY TO SEE YOU.

THOUGH IT SORELY PAINED HER TO DO SO, ELINOR LINGERED ON THE LANDING, GIVING THE LOVERS A FEW MOMENTS OF PRIVACY.

FORTITUDE, ELINOR, YOU MUST DISPLAY FORTITUDE...

SOME MINUTES LATER...

DEAR EDWARD! THIS IS A MOMENT OF GREAT HAPPINESS. THIS MIGHT ALMOST MAKE AMENDS FOR EVERYTHING.

DO YOU LIKE LONDON?

NOT AT ALL. I EXPECTED MUCH PLEASURE AND HAVE FOUND NONE. THE SIGHT OF YOU IS THE ONLY COMFORT IT HAS AFFORDED.

BUT WHY WERE YOU NOT AT YOU SISTER'S YESTERDAY?

PERHAPS HE HAD A PRIOR ENGAGEMENT. SOME GENTLEMEN KEEP THEIR ENGAGEMENTS, MISS MARIANNE, THOUGH YOU MIGHT THINK OTHERWISE.

I...ER... FEAR I MUST BE GOING.

SO SOON? THIS MUST NOT BE.

BUT EDWARD WAS DETERMINED TO FREE HIMSELF FROM THE AWKWARD SITUATION, AND LUCY DEPARTED HARD ON HIS HEELS.

HOW VEXING FOR POOR EDWARD THAT LUCY WOULD NOT LEAVE. COULD SHE NOT SEE WE WANTED HER GONE?

LUCY HAS KNOWN HIM THE LONGEST OF ANY. IT IS NATURAL HE SHOULD LIKE TO SEE HER AS WELL AS OURSELVES.

YOU KNOW, ELINOR, THAT IS A KIND OF TALKING I CANNOT BEAR.

YOU SHALL NOT TRICK ME INTO MAKING ASSURANCES YOU DO NOT WANT TO HEAR.

THE NEXT WEEK FOUND MRS. JENNINGS REPLETE WITH NEWS--NOT ONLY WAS HER DAUGHTER CHARLOTTE DELIVERED OF A HEALTHY SON, BUT SHE LEARNED OF AN INTERESTING DEVELOPMENT AT FANNY DASHWOOD'S HOME...

I BELIEVE I WOULD LIKE TO INVITE MY SISTERS HERE TO STAY.

SEVERAL GUESTS AT A PARTY THE OTHER NIGHT ASSUMED THEY WERE HERE WITH US... AND IT STARTED ME THINKING.

THE COST WOULD BE NOTHING AND IT IS THE SORT OF ATTENTION TO THEM MY FATHER WOULD HAVE APPROVED.

MY LOVE, I WOULD ASK THEM WITH ALL MY HEART. YOU KNOW I AM *ALWAYS* READY TO PAY THEM ANY ATTENTION.

BUT I HAVE JUST SETTLED WITHIN MYSELF TO ASK THE MISSES STEELE TO SPEND A FEW DAYS WITH US.

THEY ARE SO VERY WELL BEHAVED AND I THINK THE ATTENTION IS DUE TO THEM. THEIR UNCLE DID SO VERY WELL BY EDWARD, YOU RECALL.

IF YOU WISH IT, LET THEM COME.

PERHAPS WE SHALL INVITE MY SISTERS NEXT YEAR-- THOUGH IT WOULDN'T BE AMISS TO CONJECTURE THAT ELINOR MAY BE HERE AS COLONEL BRANDON'S WIFE AND MARIANNE AS *THEIR* VISITOR.

LUCY, NATURALLY, LOST NO TIME IN RELAYING THE NEWS TO ELINOR.

MRS. DASHWOOD WROTE TO INVITE US ONLY THIS MORNING... SHE VOWS SHE HAS NEVER BEEN AS PLEASED WITH ANY YOUNG WOMEN IN HER LIFE.

IT IS A MARK OF UNCOMMON KINDNESS ON HER PART.

SUCH A CHANCE TO BE WITH EDWARD AND HIS FAMILY IS ABOVE ALL THINGS WONDERFUL. THIS IS MOST GRATIFYING TO MY FEELINGS.

HER FLATTERY HAS ALREADY SUBDUED THE PRIDE OF LADY MIDDLETON AND MADE ENTRY INTO THE CLOSE HEART OF FANNY. WHO KNOWS HOW FAR IT SHALL CARRY HER?

BUT LUCY'S BRIGHT PROSPECTS WERE SHORTLIVED, ALAS...

OH, MY DEARS, WHAT A TANGLE!

AS I WAS LEAVING CHARLOTTE'S SHE TOLD ME...THAT IF MY YOUNG CHARGES SHOULD HEAR THAT THEIR SISTER IS AILING, THERE IS NO REASON FOR ALARM.

THAT SHE EXPECTS MRS. DASHWOOD WILL DO VERY WELL.

IS FANNY ILL?

THAT IS EXACTLY WHAT I ASKED. LORD, NO, SAYS CHARLOTTE. JUST OUT OF TEMPER.

IT'S ALL TO DO WITH MR. FERRARS, WHO I USED TO JOKE ABOUT WITH YOU, ELINOR...IT SEEMS HE HAS BEEN SECRETLY ENGAGED TO MY COUSIN LUCY STEELE.

NOT A SOUL KNEW ABOUT IT BUT ANNE. I HAD NEVER SEEN THEM TOGETHER OR I SHOULD HAVE FOUND IT OUT AT ONCE.

EDWARD *ENGAGED?* THIS CANNOT BE!

OF COURSE, NEITHER YOUR BROTHER NOR FANNY SUSPECTED ANYTHING... TILL THIS MORNING, WHEN ANNE-- WHO IS WELL MEANING, BUT NO CONJURER--POPT IT ALL OUT.

FANNY FELL INTO VIOLENT HYSTERICS IMMEDIATELY, WITH SUCH SCREAMS THAT YOUR BROTHER FLEW TO THE ROOM.

LUCY CAME IN THEN AND THERE WAS A TERRIBLE SCENE, WITH FANNY SCOLDING HER LIKE A FURY.

POOR LUCY, I DO PITY HER. SHE WAS DRIVEN INTO A FAINTING FIT, WHILE ANNE FELL TO HER KNEES CRYING AS FANNY VOWED THEY MUST LEAVE THE HOUSE THAT INSTANT.

YOUR BROTHER PLEADED WITH HER TO AT LEAST ALLOW THEM TO PACK THEIR BAGS. CAN YOU IMAGINE? I DECLARE, I HAVE NO PATIENCE WITH YOUR SISTER.

I BELIEVE FANNY AND MRS. FERRARS HAD LORD MORTON'S DAUGHTER IN MIND FOR EDWARD.

SOME PEOPLE MAKE *SUCH* A TO-DO ABOUT MONEY AND GREATNESS. WHY SHOULDN'T LUCY AND EDWARD MAKE A MATCH OF IT?

AH, I MUST LIE DOWN...MY NERVES ARE QUITE UNSETTLED.

*A*FTER THEIR HOSTESS DEPARTED, MARIANNE FLEW TO ELINOR'S SIDE.

ARE YOU IN *SHOCK,* THAT YOU SAY SO LITTLE? YOU SEE ME IN TEARS AT THE NEWS--EDWARD A SECOND WILLOUGHBY!-- AND YET YOU REMAIN CALM.

I AM SO SORRY YOU HAVE LOST ONE OF YOUR CHIEF CONSOLATIONS-- EDWARD'S GOOD CHARACTER-- AND PRAY HE HAS NOT FOREVER FORFEITED YOUR FAVOR.

FOR MYSELF, I CAN VINDICATE EDWARD OF EVERY CHARGE SAVE IMPRUDENCE.

AND, NO, I AM NOT SHOCKED BY THE NEWS. LUCY CONFIDED IN ME FOUR MONTHS AGO.

FOUR MONTHS! WHAT!--WHILE ATTENDING *ME* IN ALL *MY* MISERY, THIS HAD BEEN IN *YOUR* HEART? AND I HAVE REPROACHED *YOU* FOR BEING HAPPY...

IT WAS NOT FIT THAT YOU SHOULD KNOW HOW MUCH I WAS THE REVERSE.

FOUR MONTHS! SO CALM, SO CHEERFUL-- HOW HAVE YOU BEEN SUPPORTED?

BY FEELING I WAS DOING MY DUTY. I OWED IT TO MY FRIENDS AND FAMILY NOT TO CREATE IN THEM A SOLICITUDE ABOUT ME THAT WAS NOT IN MY POWER TO SATISFY.

YET YOU LOVED HIM.

YES. BUT I DID NOT LOVE ONLY HIM. AND AS LONG AS THE COMFORT OF OTHERS WAS DEAR TO ME, I WAS GLAD TO SPARE THEM FROM KNOWING HOW I FELT.

I WOULD NOT HAVE YOU SUFFER ON MY ACCOUNT, FOR I ASSURE YOU I NO LONGER SUFFER MATERIALLY MYSELF.

IF THIS IS YOUR WAY OF THINKING, IF THE LOSS OF WHAT YOU VALUED IS SO EASILY TO BE MADE UP BY SOMETHING ELSE, YOUR RESOLUTION, YOUR SELF-COMMAND, ARE, PERHAPS, A LITTLE LESS TO BE WONDERED AT.

THEY ARE BROUGHT MORE WITHIN MY COMPREHENSION.

I ACQUIT EDWARD OF ESSENTIAL MISCONDUCT. I WISH HIM TO BE VERY HAPPY; I AM SO SURE OF EDWARD ALWAYS DOING HIS DUTY, THAT THOUGH NOW HE MAY HARBOR SOME REGRET, IN THE END HE WILL BECOME SO.

HE WILL MARRY LUCY, A WOMAN SUPERIOR IN UNDERSTANDING TO HALF HER SEX. AND TIME WILL TEACH HIM TO FORGET HE EVER THOUGHT ANOTHER WOMAN SUPERIOR TO *HER*.

YOU DO NOT SUPPOSE THAT I HAVE EVER FELT MUCH. YET FOR *FOUR MONTHS* THIS HAS BEEN HANGING ON MY MIND, WITHOUT THE LIBERTY TO TELL A SOUL.

THIS CONFIDENCE, FORCED ON ME--IN TRIUMPH-- BY THE *VERY PERSON* WHOSE PRIOR ENGAGEMENT RUINED ALL MY PROSPECTS. I HAVE HAD TO ALLAY HER SUSPICIONS BY APPEARING INDIFFERENT WHERE I HAVE BEEN MOST DEEPLY INTERESTED.

I HAVE FOUND MYSELF DIVIDED FROM EDWARD FOREVER...WITHOUT HEARING ONE CIRCUMSTANCE THAT COULD MAKE ME DESIRE THE CONNECTION LESS.

NOTHING HAS PROVED HIM UNWORTHY, NOR HAS ANYTHING DECLARED HIM INDIFFERENT TO ME.

I HAVE HAD TO CONTEND AGAINST THE UNKINDNESS OF HIS SISTER, THE INTOLERANCE OF HIS MOTHER, AND SUFFERED ALL THE PUNISHMENT OF AN ATTACHMENT AND NONE OF THE ADVANTAGES.

AND ALL THIS HAS BEEN GOING ON AT A TIME WHEN, YOU WELL KNOW, IT HAS NOT BEEN MY ONLY UNHAPPINESS.

IF YOU CAN THINK ME EVER CAPABLE OF FEELING, SURELY YOU MAY SUPPOSE THAT I HAVE SUFFERED *NOW*.

OH, ELINOR! YOU HAVE MADE ME HATE MYSELF FOREVER. HOW BARBAROUS I HAVE BEEN TO YOU. YOU, WHO HAVE BEEN MY ONLY COMFORT. IS THIS MY GRATITUDE?

HOW BLIND I WAS TO THINK YOU WERE ONLY SUFFERING FOR ME.

PLEASE FORGIVE ME. YOUR MERIT CRIES OUT UPON MYSELF, AND YET I HAVE BEEN TRYING TO THRUST IT AWAY.

THE NEXT MORNING BROUGHT ANOTHER TRIAL--A VISIT BY THEIR BROTHER.

YOU WILL HAVE HEARD OF THE SHOCKING DISCOVERY THAT TOOK PLACE UNDER OUR ROOF YESTERDAY. YOUR SISTER AND MRS. FERRARS HAVE SUFFERED **DREADFULLY...**

ACH, THE *INGRATITUDE* OF THOSE GIRLS!

POOR FANNY WAS IN HYSTERICS ALL DAY, YET SHE HAS BORNE IT ALL WITH THE FORTITUDE OF AN ANGEL.

MRS. FERRARS, UPON HEARING THE TALE, CALLED EDWARD TO HER. HE CAME, BUT I AM SORRY TO RELATE WHAT ENSUED.

ALL SHE COULD SAY TO MAKE HIM PUT AN END TO THE ENGAGEMENT, AIDED BY MY ARGUMENTS AND FANNIE'S ENTREATIES, WAS OF NO AVAIL.

DUTY, AFFECTION, *EVERYTHING* WAS DISREGARDED.

SHE EVEN REMINDED HIM THAT CERTAIN PENURY MUST ATTEND THE MATCH AND THAT IF HE WERE TO ENTER ANY PROFESSION, SHE WOULD DO ALL IN HER POWER TO PREVENT HIM ADVANCING IN IT.

GRACIOUS GOD! CAN THIS BE *POSSIBLE*?

YES, MARIANNE, YOU MAY WONDER AT THE OBSTINACY WHICH COULD RESIST SUCH ARGUMENTS.

THAT'S NOT WHAT--

ALL THIS, HOWEVER, WAS URGED IN VAIN. *NOTHING* COULD PREVAIL UPON EDWARD TO END HIS ENGAGEMENT.

HE WOULD STAND TO IT, COST HIM WHAT IT MIGHT.

THEN HE HAS ACTED LIKE AN HONEST MAN. I BEG YOUR PARDON, MR. DASHWOOD, BUT IF HE HAD DONE OTHERWISE, I SHOULD HAVE THOUGHT HIM A RASCAL.

I HAVE SOME LITTLE CONCERN IN THE BUSINESS--LUCY STEELE IS MY COUSIN, AND THERE IS NOT A BETTER GIRL IN THE WORLD.

I WOULD NOT SPEAK DISRESPECTFULLY OF YOUR RELATION, MA'AM, BUT IN THIS CASE YOU KNOW THE CONNECTION MUST BE IMPOSSIBLE.

I DARESAY YOUR COUSIN IS A DESERVING YOUNG WOMAN, BUT TO HAVE ENTERED INTO A SECRET ENGAGEMENT WITH THE SON OF A WOMAN WITH A VERY LARGE FORTUNE IS...A LITTLE EXTRAORDINARY.

MRS. FERRARS' CONDUCT THROUGHOUT HAS BEEN DIGNIFIED AND LIBERAL. EDWARD HAS DRAWN HIS OWN LOT AND I FEAR IT WILL BE A BAD ONE.

WELL, SIR, HOW DID IT END?

I AM SORRY TO SAY, MA'AM, IN A MOST UNHAPPY RUPTURE.

EDWARD IS DISMISSED FOREVER FROM HIS MOTHER'S NOTICE. HE LEFT HER HOUSE AND WE DO NOT KNOW WHERE HE HAS GONE.

ROBERT IS NOW FOR ALL INTENTS THE ELDEST SON AND HEIR...AND SHALL LIKELY MARRY MISS MORTON.

WELL, THAT IS HER REVENGE. EVERYBODY HAS A WAY OF THEIR OWN.

SEVERAL DAYS LATER, ELINOR WAS WALKING IN KENSINGTON GARDENS WITH HER HOSTESS WHEN SHE WAS ACCOSTED BY ANNE STEELE.

I SUPPOSE MRS. JENNINGS HAS HEARD ALL ABOUT IT. IS SHE ANGRY...IS LADY MIDDLETON ANGRY?

OH, IT DOESN'T MATTER...I AM MONSTROUS GLAD OF IT. LUCY WAS IN SUCH A RAGE AT ME FOR LETTING HER SECRET OUT...BUT NOW SHE HAS FORGIVEN ME AND WE ARE AS GOOD FRIENDS AS EVER.

HOW IS SHE FARING THROUGH ALL THE TURMOIL?

NOT WELL, AT FIRST. EDWARD DID NOT COME TO US FOR THREE DAYS AFTER THE SCENE WITH MRS. DASHWOOD.

HOWEVER, HE MET US THIS MORNING JUST AS WE RETURNED FROM CHURCH. HE HAD RID INTO THE COUNTRY, TO THINK OVER HIS PROSPECTS.

HE SAID IT SEEMED TO HIM AS IF, NOW HE HAD NO FORTUNE, AND NO NOTHING AT ALL, IT WOULD BE QUITE UNKIND TO HOLD LUCY TO THE ENGAGEMENT.

IF HE WAS TO GO INTO ORDERS, AS HE HAS HAD SOME THOUGHTS OF DOING, HE COULD GET NOTHING BUT A CURACY, AND HOW WOULD THEY LIVE UPON THAT?

HE COULD NOT BEAR TO THINK OF LUCY DOING NO BETTER, AND SO HE BEGGED HER TO PUT AN END TO THE MATTER DIRECTLY.

LUCY WOULD NOT HEAR OF SUCH A THING. SHE TOLD HIM DIRECTLY SHE COULD LIVE WITH HIM ON A TRIFLE OR HOWEVER LITTLE HE MIGHT HAVE. AND THEN HE WAS MONSTROUS HAPPY.

HE TOLD HER HE WOULD TAKE ORDERS AND THEY MUST WAIT TO MARRY UNTIL HE GOT A LIVING. AND THAT IS ALL I HEARD, FOR MY COUSIN CALLED FOR HER FROM THE HALLWAY, AND I HAD TO GO IN AND INTERRUPT THEM.

WHAT DO YOU MEAN INTERRUPT THEM? YOU WERE NOT IN THE ROOM WITH THEM?

OH, LA, MISS DASHWOOD, DO YOU THINK PEOPLE MAKE LOVE WHEN ANYBODY ELSE IS BY? NO, THEY WERE IN THE DRAWING ROOM TOGETHER AND I WAS LISTENING AT THE DOOR.

YOU--YOU HAVE BEEN REPEATING TO ME A PRIVATE CONVERSATION YOU OVERHEARD BY EAVESDROPPING?

I CERTAINLY WOULD NOT HAVE SUFFERED YOU TO GIVE ME THE DETAILS HAD I KNOWN THAT. HOW COULD YOU BEHAVE SO UNFAIRLY TO YOUR SISTER?

LUCY LISTENS IN ON ME ALL THE TIME.

OH, LOOK, THERE ARE MY FRIENDS. I MUST BE OFF.

WHAT A PITY... I HAD SO MUCH MORE TO TELL YOU, MISS DASHWOOD.

WHEN QUESTIONED BY MRS. JENNINGS, ELINOR RELAYED ONLY THE SIMPLE PARTICULARS OF ANNE'S TALE, THOSE THAT LUCY HERSELF MIGHT CHOOSE TO HAVE KNOWN.

...AND SO EDWARD IS TO TAKE ORDERS AND BECOME A CURATE.

TAKING ORDERS! WAITING TO HAVE A LIVING! WE ALL KNOW HOW THAT WILL END.

THEY WILL WAIT A TWELVEMONTH, SETTLE FOR A CURACY OF FIFTY POUNDS A YEAR...THEN THEY WILL HAVE A CHILD EVERY YEAR--

AND LORD HELP THEM, HOW POOR THEY WILL BE!

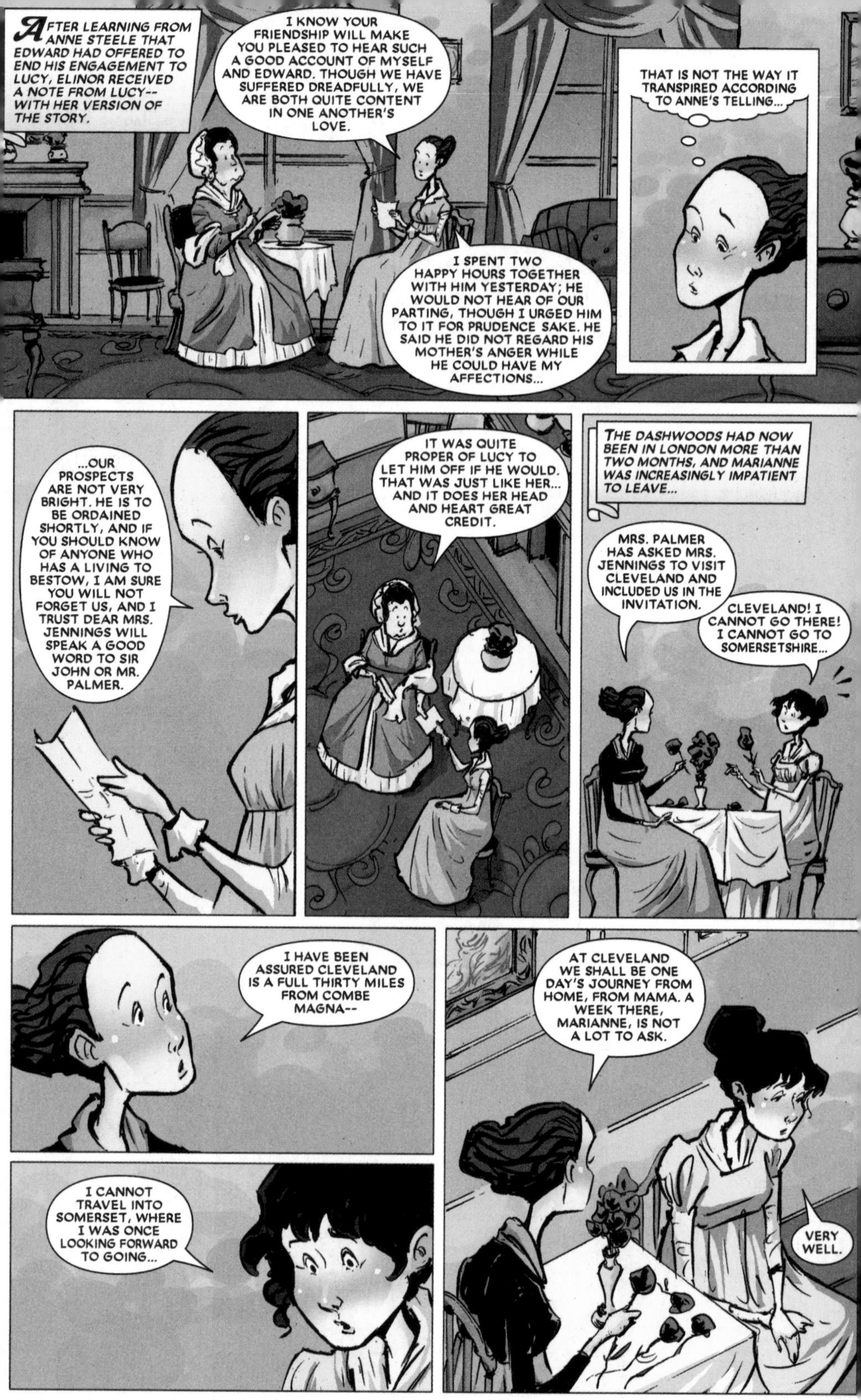
AFTER LEARNING FROM ANNE STEELE THAT EDWARD HAD OFFERED TO END HIS ENGAGEMENT TO LUCY, ELINOR RECEIVED A NOTE FROM LUCY-- WITH HER VERSION OF THE STORY.
I KNOW YOUR FRIENDSHIP WILL MAKE YOU PLEASED TO HEAR SUCH A GOOD ACCOUNT OF MYSELF AND EDWARD. THOUGH WE HAVE SUFFERED DREADFULLY, WE ARE BOTH QUITE CONTENT IN ONE ANOTHER'S LOVE.
I SPENT TWO HAPPY HOURS TOGETHER WITH HIM YESTERDAY; HE WOULD NOT HEAR OF OUR PARTING, THOUGH I URGED HIM TO IT FOR PRUDENCE SAKE. HE SAID HE DID NOT REGARD HIS MOTHER'S ANGER WHILE HE COULD HAVE MY AFFECTIONS...
THAT IS NOT THE WAY IT TRANSPIRED ACCORDING TO ANNE'S TELLING...
...OUR PROSPECTS ARE NOT VERY BRIGHT. HE IS TO BE ORDAINED SHORTLY, AND IF YOU SHOULD KNOW OF ANYONE WHO HAS A LIVING TO BESTOW, I AM SURE YOU WILL NOT FORGET US, AND I TRUST DEAR MRS. JENNINGS WILL SPEAK A GOOD WORD TO SIR JOHN OR MR. PALMER.
IT WAS QUITE PROPER OF LUCY TO LET HIM OFF IF HE WOULD. THAT WAS JUST LIKE HER... AND IT DOES HER HEAD AND HEART GREAT CREDIT.
THE DASHWOODS HAD NOW BEEN IN LONDON MORE THAN TWO MONTHS, AND MARIANNE WAS INCREASINGLY IMPATIENT TO LEAVE...
MRS. PALMER HAS ASKED MRS. JENNINGS TO VISIT CLEVELAND AND INCLUDED US IN THE INVITATION.
CLEVELAND! I CANNOT GO THERE! I CANNOT GO TO SOMERSETSHIRE...
I HAVE BEEN ASSURED CLEVELAND IS A FULL THIRTY MILES FROM COMBE MAGNA--
I CANNOT TRAVEL INTO SOMERSET, WHERE I WAS ONCE LOOKING FORWARD TO GOING...
AT CLEVELAND WE SHALL BE ONE DAY'S JOURNEY FROM HOME, FROM MAMA. A WEEK THERE, MARIANNE, IS NOT A LOT TO ASK.
VERY WELL.

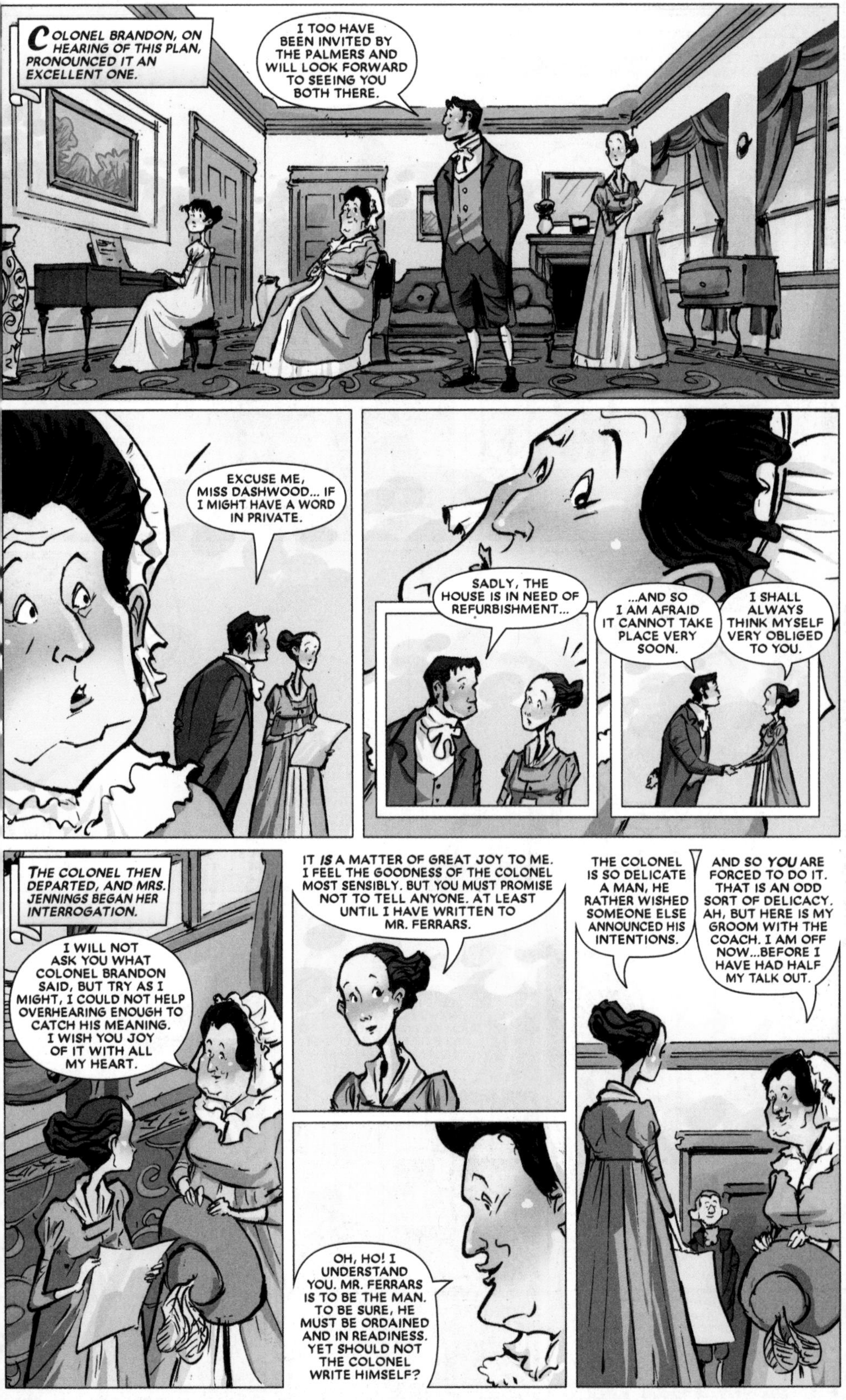
COLONEL BRANDON, ON HEARING OF THIS PLAN, PRONOUNCED IT AN EXCELLENT ONE.
I TOO HAVE BEEN INVITED BY THE PALMERS AND WILL LOOK FORWARD TO SEEING YOU BOTH THERE.
EXCUSE ME, MISS DASHWOOD... IF I MIGHT HAVE A WORD IN PRIVATE.
SADLY, THE HOUSE IS IN NEED OF REFURBISHMENT...
...AND SO I AM AFRAID IT CANNOT TAKE PLACE VERY SOON.
I SHALL ALWAYS THINK MYSELF VERY OBLIGED TO YOU.
THE COLONEL THEN DEPARTED, AND MRS. JENNINGS BEGAN HER INTERROGATION.
I WILL NOT ASK YOU WHAT COLONEL BRANDON SAID, BUT TRY AS I MIGHT, I COULD NOT HELP OVERHEARING ENOUGH TO CATCH HIS MEANING. I WISH YOU JOY OF IT WITH ALL MY HEART.
IT *IS* A MATTER OF GREAT JOY TO ME. I FEEL THE GOODNESS OF THE COLONEL MOST SENSIBLY. BUT YOU MUST PROMISE NOT TO TELL ANYONE. AT LEAST UNTIL I HAVE WRITTEN TO MR. FERRARS.
OH, HO! I UNDERSTAND YOU. MR. FERRARS IS TO BE THE MAN. TO BE SURE, HE MUST BE ORDAINED AND IN READINESS. YET SHOULD NOT THE COLONEL WRITE HIMSELF?
THE COLONEL IS SO DELICATE A MAN, HE RATHER WISHED SOMEONE ELSE ANNOUNCED HIS INTENTIONS.
AND SO *YOU* ARE FORCED TO DO IT. THAT IS AN ODD SORT OF DELICACY. AH, BUT HERE IS MY GROOM WITH THE COACH. I AM OFF NOW...BEFORE I HAVE HAD HALF MY TALK OUT.

ONCE SHE WAS ALONE, ELINOR SAT DOWN TO WRITE TO EDWARD, TO RELATE WHAT THE COLONEL HAD TOLD HER.

MR. FERRARS, MA'AM.

MRS. JENNINGS STOPPED ME ON THE STREET AND TOLD ME YOU WISHED TO SPEAK WITH ME. I...I AM GLAD FOR THE OPPORTUNITY TO SEE YOU BEFORE I LEAVE FOR OXFORD IN THE MORNING.

MRS. JENNINGS WAS CORRECT. I HAVE SOMETHING OF CONSEQUENCE TO TELL YOU. INDEED, I AM CHARGED WITH A MOST AGREEABLE OFFICE.

COLONEL BRANDON, WHO WAS HERE NOT TEN MINUTES AGO, HAS DESIRED ME TO SAY--UNDERSTANDING YOU MEAN TO TAKE ORDERS--HE HAS THE GREAT PLEASURE OF OFFERING YOU THE LIVING AT DELAFORD.

COLONEL BRANDON!

YES. HE MEANS IT AS A TESTIMONY OF HIS CONCERN FOR WHAT HAS LATELY PASSED-- FOR THE CRUEL SITUATION IN WHICH THE UNJUSTIFIABLE CONDUCT OF YOUR FAMILY HAS PLACED YOU. A CONCERN WHICH ALL YOUR FRIENDS SHARE.

COLONEL BRANDON GIVE ME A LIVING! CAN IT BE POSSIBLE?

THE UNKINDNESS OF YOUR OWN RELATIONS MAKES YOU ASTONISHED TO FIND FRIENDSHIP ANYWHERE.

NO, NOT TO FIND IT IN YOU.

YET IT IS TRUE. HE WISHES IT WERE MORE VALUABLE, MORE CONSIDERABLE, SUCH AS WOULD ALLOW YOU TO ESTABLISH ALL YOUR VIEWS OF HAPPINESS-- IT IS ABOUT TWO HUNDRED POUNDS A YEAR.

I CANNOT BE IGNORANT THAT TO YOU, TO YOUR GOODNESS, I OWE IT ALL.

COLONEL BRANDON SEEMS A MAN OF GREAT WORTH AND RESPECTABILITY. IF YOU WILL GIVE ME HIS DIRECTION, I WILL GO AT ONCE TO HIS HOUSE AND THANK HIM.

GOOD BYE, DEAR FRIEND.

WHEN I SEE HIM AGAIN, I SHALL SEE THE HUSBAND OF LUCY.

*M*RS. JENNINGS RETURNED HOME PLEASED TO HAVE ENGINEERED THE MEETING.

WELL, MY DEAR, DID I DO WELL TO SEND HIM TO YOU? HOW SOON WILL HE BE READY?

I CAN HARDLY CONJECTURE. I SUPPOSE IT MIGHT TAKE TWO OR THREE MONTHS TO COMPLETE HIS ORDINATION.

THAT LONG? CAN THE COLONEL WAIT TWO OR THREE MONTHS? SURELY THERE IS ANOTHER WHO CAN BE FOUND TO PERFORM THE CEREMONY AS WELL. I HARDLY THINK COLONEL BRANDON WANTS TO DELAY HIS MARRIAGE TO YOU FOR THE SAKE OF GIVING TEN GUINEAS TO EDWARD FERRARS!

GOOD HEAVENS, MA'AM. THE COLONEL IS NOT OFFERING MARRIAGE TO *ME*, HE IS OFFERING THE LIVING AT DELAFORD TO MR. FERRARS.

WELL, BLESS MY STARS! WHO COULD HAVE GUESSED? AH, BUT I MUST TRADE ONE FORM OF DELIGHT FOR ANOTHER. NOW EDWARD AND MY DEAR LUCY CAN MARRY.

THE COLONEL SEEMED TO THINK THE LIVING WAS NOT ADEQUATE FOR TWO.

COLONEL BRANDON IS A NINNY. HE THINKS THAT BECAUSE HE HAS TWO THOUSAND A YEAR THAT NO ONE CAN MARRY ON LESS.

TAKE MY WORD FOR IT--I SHALL BE VISITING LUCY AT DELAFORD PARSONAGE BY MICHAELMAS.

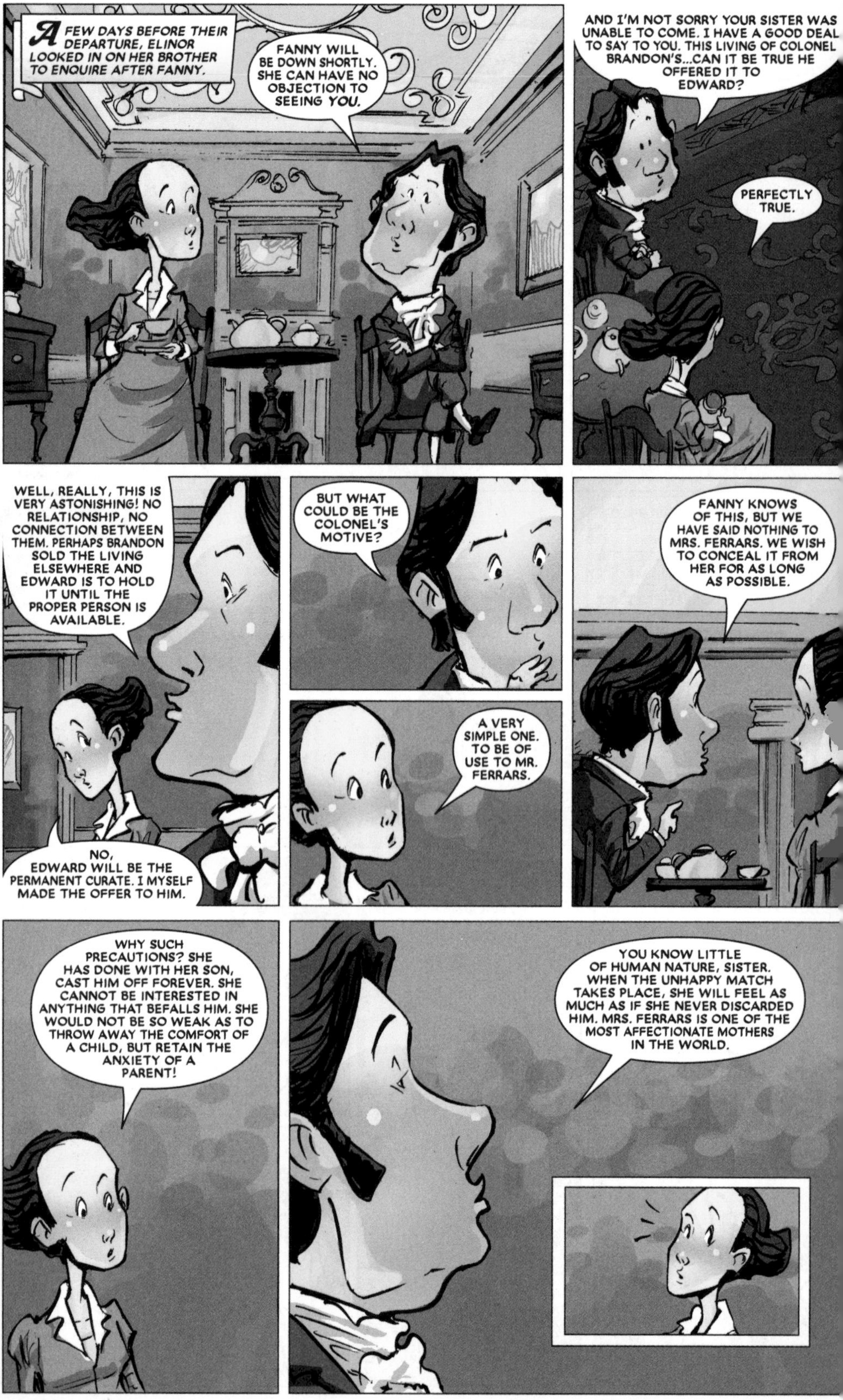
A FEW DAYS BEFORE THEIR DEPARTURE, ELINOR LOOKED IN ON HER BROTHER TO ENQUIRE AFTER FANNY.
FANNY WILL BE DOWN SHORTLY. SHE CAN HAVE NO OBJECTION TO SEEING YOU.
AND I'M NOT SORRY YOUR SISTER WAS UNABLE TO COME. I HAVE A GOOD DEAL TO SAY TO YOU. THIS LIVING OF COLONEL BRANDON'S...CAN IT BE TRUE HE OFFERED IT TO EDWARD?
PERFECTLY TRUE.
WELL, REALLY, THIS IS VERY ASTONISHING! NO RELATIONSHIP, NO CONNECTION BETWEEN THEM. PERHAPS BRANDON SOLD THE LIVING ELSEWHERE AND EDWARD IS TO HOLD IT UNTIL THE PROPER PERSON IS AVAILABLE.
NO, EDWARD WILL BE THE PERMANENT CURATE. I MYSELF MADE THE OFFER TO HIM.
BUT WHAT COULD BE THE COLONEL'S MOTIVE?
A VERY SIMPLE ONE. TO BE OF USE TO MR. FERRARS.
FANNY KNOWS OF THIS, BUT WE HAVE SAID NOTHING TO MRS. FERRARS. WE WISH TO CONCEAL IT FROM HER FOR AS LONG AS POSSIBLE.
WHY SUCH PRECAUTIONS? SHE HAS DONE WITH HER SON, CAST HIM OFF FOREVER. SHE CANNOT BE INTERESTED IN ANYTHING THAT BEFALLS HIM. SHE WOULD NOT BE SO WEAK AS TO THROW AWAY THE COMFORT OF A CHILD, BUT RETAIN THE ANXIETY OF A PARENT!
YOU KNOW LITTLE OF HUMAN NATURE, SISTER. WHEN THE UNHAPPY MATCH TAKES PLACE, SHE WILL FEEL AS MUCH AS IF SHE NEVER DISCARDED HIM. MRS. FERRARS IS ONE OF THE MOST AFFECTIONATE MOTHERS IN THE WORLD.

OF *ONE* THING, I MAY ASSURE YOU. I HAVE IT FROM MRS. FERRARS--WELL, FROM HER DAUGHTER--THAT WHATEVER OBJECTIONS SHE DID HAVE TO A CERTAIN CONNECTION-- YOU UNDERSTAND ME-- IT WOULD HAVE BEEN FAR PREFERABLE TO HER THAN THIS VEXATION.

SHE SAID, IN FACT, THAT IT WOULD HAVE BEEN THE LEAST EVIL OF THE TWO.

I HARDLY KNOW WHAT TO SAY...

HO, ROBERT. HAVE YOU MET MY SISTER, ELINOR? WE WERE JUST SPEAKING OF EDWARD. LET ME GO UP AND FETCH FANNY. SHE WON'T WANT TO MISS YOU.

AH, POOR EDWARD. THE IDEA OF HIS BEING A CLERGYMAN IS DIVERTING BEYOND ALL MEASURE, READING PRAYERS IN A WHITE SURPLICE. WE MAY TREAT IT AS A JOKE, BUT IT IS MOST SERIOUS. HE IS RUINED FOREVER.

I KNOW HIM TO BE A GOOD-HEARTED CREATURE. YOU MUST NOT JUDGE HIM ON YOUR SLIGHT ACQUAINTANCE, MISS DASHWOOD. HIS MANNERS ARE NOT THE HAPPIEST IN NATURE, BUT WE ARE NOT ALL BORN WITH THE SAME POWERS, THE SAME ADDRESS.

WHEN MY MOTHER TOLD ME OF IT, I REMARKED THAT IF EDWARD DOES MARRY THIS WOMAN, I SHALL NEVER SEE HIM AGAIN.

HAVE YOU EVER SEEN THE LADY?

YES. WHILE SHE WAS STAYING HERE, I DROPPED IN FOR TEN MINUTES AND SAW QUITE ENOUGH. THE MEREST AWKWARD COUNTRY GIRL, WITHOUT STYLE OR ELEGANCE, ALMOST WITHOUT BEAUTY. HAD I KNOWN OF THE MATTER BEFORE IT WAS ANNOUNCED, I SHOULD CERTAINLY HAVE TALKED HIM OUT OF IT.

AH, BUT LOOK, HERE'S FANNY...

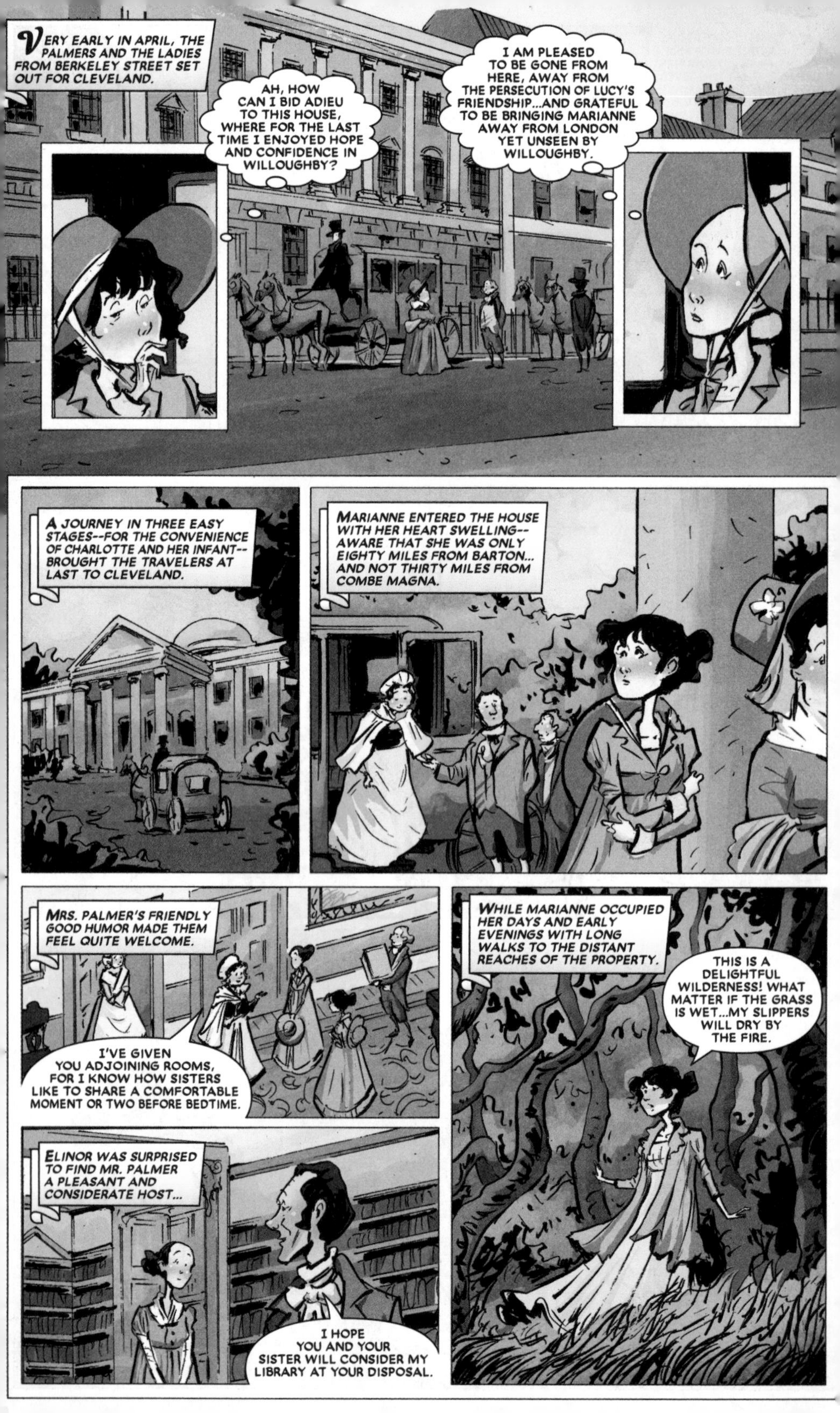
VERY EARLY IN APRIL, THE PALMERS AND THE LADIES FROM BERKELEY STREET SET OUT FOR CLEVELAND.
AH, HOW CAN I BID ADIEU TO THIS HOUSE, WHERE FOR THE LAST TIME I ENJOYED HOPE AND CONFIDENCE IN WILLOUGHBY?
I AM PLEASED TO BE GONE FROM HERE, AWAY FROM THE PERSECUTION OF LUCY'S FRIENDSHIP...AND GRATEFUL TO BE BRINGING MARIANNE AWAY FROM LONDON YET UNSEEN BY WILLOUGHBY.
A JOURNEY IN THREE EASY STAGES--FOR THE CONVENIENCE OF CHARLOTTE AND HER INFANT--BROUGHT THE TRAVELERS AT LAST TO CLEVELAND.
MARIANNE ENTERED THE HOUSE WITH HER HEART SWELLING--AWARE THAT SHE WAS ONLY EIGHTY MILES FROM BARTON... AND NOT THIRTY MILES FROM COMBE MAGNA.
MRS. PALMER'S FRIENDLY GOOD HUMOR MADE THEM FEEL QUITE WELCOME.
I'VE GIVEN YOU ADJOINING ROOMS, FOR I KNOW HOW SISTERS LIKE TO SHARE A COMFORTABLE MOMENT OR TWO BEFORE BEDTIME.
ELINOR WAS SURPRISED TO FIND MR. PALMER A PLEASANT AND CONSIDERATE HOST...
I HOPE YOU AND YOUR SISTER WILL CONSIDER MY LIBRARY AT YOUR DISPOSAL.
WHILE MARIANNE OCCUPIED HER DAYS AND EARLY EVENINGS WITH LONG WALKS TO THE DISTANT REACHES OF THE PROPERTY.
THIS IS A DELIGHTFUL WILDERNESS! WHAT MATTER IF THE GRASS IS WET...MY SLIPPERS WILL DRY BY THE FIRE.

ALAS, ON THE FIFTH DAY OF HER VISIT TO CLEVELAND, MARIANNE CAME DOWN WITH A VIOLENT COLD.

PLEASE DRINK IT. I ASKED COOK TO MAKE IT UP SPECIAL.

COUGH! COUGH!

THE NEXT MORNING...

I'M AFRAID I'M...TOO WEAK TO SIT UP.

I'D BETTER ASK MR. PALMER TO SEND FOR THE APOTHECARY.

I EXPECT A FEW DAYS REST WILL RESTORE HER TO HEALTH. SHE IS SUFFERING AN INFECTION OF THE THROAT, PERHAPS WITH A PUTRID TENDENCY.

INFECTION! GOOD HEAVENS! I MUST REMOVE MY SON FROM THIS HOUSE INSTANTLY. WE SHALL GO TO MR. PALMER'S COUSIN IN BATH.

GO AND PACK, CHARLOTTE. I WILL ALERT HIS NURSE TO HAVE HIM READY TO TRAVEL WITHIN THE HOUR.

SEVERAL DAYS PASSED AND MARIANNE WAS NO BETTER.

WE WERE TO HAVE RETURNED HOME TODAY, ELINOR. WE WERE GOING TO SURPRISE MAMA.

DON'T FRET, DEAREST. IT WILL ONLY BE A SHORT DELAY.

AS MR. PALMER WAS LEAVING TO JOIN HIS WIFE, COLONEL BRANDON ALSO TALKED OF GOING HOME...

MISS DASHWOOD IS MUCH TROUBLED BY HER SISTER'S ILLNESS... I DON'T WANT MY BEING HERE TO CAUSE HER ANY ADDITIONAL CONCERN.

NONSENSE, COLONEL. MISS DASHWOOD MIGHT REQUIRE YOUR SERVICES... AND FOR MYSELF, I WOULD BE HAPPY FOR A PIQUET PARTNER IN THE EVENINGS.

INDEED, MA'AM, MY STRONGEST INCLINATION IS TO STAY.

YES, PLEASE STAY. IT WILL EASE MY MIND, KNOWING THERE IS AN ABLE MAN ABOUT THE PLACE.

BY THE THIRD DAY, MARIANNE APPEARED TO BE RECOVERING. BUT LATER THAT NIGHT.

MAMA! IS MAMA COMING?

SHE MUST NOT GO ROUND BY LONDON. I SHALL NEVER SEE HER IF SHE GOES BY LONDON!

SHSSSH... SHE IS COMING, MARIANNE. YOU SHALL SEE HER SOON.

ELINOR WAS NOW TRULY ALARMED FOR HER SISTER.

I HEARD YOUR SISTER CRYING OUT.

SHE HAS TAKEN A TURN FOR THE WORSE. WE NEED TO SEND FOR MR. HARRIS AT ONCE. AND I THINK WE MUST DISPATCH A MESSENGER TO MY MOTHER TO FETCH HER HERE.

IT WOULD GIVE ME GREAT PLEASURE TO BE THAT MESSENGER.

I...I CANNOT EXPRESS MY GRATITUDE. YOUR PRESENCE WILL EASE THE SHOCK OF THE SUMMONS.

I FEAR THIS WAS BROUGHT ON BY HER GREAT DISAPPOINTMENT IN LONDON.

I THINK YOU MIGHT BE RIGHT. HER SPIRITS HAVE SUFFERED FOR SO MANY WEEKS.

TWO DAYS PASSED WITH NO ALTERATION IN MARIANNE'S CONDITION, BUT THEN...

ELINOR... I...I'M FEELING A LITTLE BETTER.

DEAREST SISTER... JUST TO HEAR YOU SAY MY NAME. YOU HAVEN'T KNOWN ME FOR DAYS. BUT I BELIEVE YOUR FEVER HAS FINALLY BROKEN.

MR. HARRIS DECLARED MARIANNE OUT OF DANGER. ELINOR SPENT THE AFTERNOON NAPPING, AND WHEN SHE AWOKE, IT WAS TO A FIERCE STORM.

ARE THOSE CARRIAGE LIGHTS?

COLONEL BRANDON IS DUE BACK AT ANY TIME... AH, MAMA WILL BE SO RELIEVED TO HEAR MARIANNE IS ON THE MEND.

PLEASE, MISS DASHWOOD...A HALF HOUR, TEN MINUTES. I ENTREAT YOU TO STAY.

I SHALL NOT STAY. YOUR BUSINESS CANNOT BE WITH ME. HAVE THE SERVANTS NOT TOLD YOU MR. PALMER IS AWAY FROM HOME?

MR. PALMER AND ALL HIS RELATIONS COULD BE AT THE DEVIL, IT WILL NOT TURN ME FROM THIS DOOR. MY BUSINESS IS WITH YOU.

WELL, WILLOUGHBY, BE QUICK--AND IF YOU CAN--LESS VIOLENT.

YOUR SISTER IS OUT OF DANGER. I HEARD IT FROM THE FOOTMAN. GOD BE PRAISED! BUT IS IT TRUE?

WE... WE HOPE SHE IS.

HAD I KNOWN AS MUCH AN HOUR AGO...BUT SINCE I AM HERE, LET US BE CHEERFUL TOGETHER. I AM IN A FINE MOOD FOR GAITY. AH, DON'T GAZE AT ME SO.

YES, I AM VERY DRUNK. I DROVE STRAIGHT FROM LONDON AND ONLY STOPPED FOR A PINT OF PORTER, ENOUGH TO OVERSET ME.

MR. WILLOUGHBY, AFTER WHAT HAS PASSED, YOUR COMING HERE IN THIS MANNER, FORCING YOURSELF ON MY NOTICE, REQUIRES A VERY PARTICULAR EXCUSE. WHAT DO YOU MEAN BY IT?

I MEAN TO MAKE YOU HATE ME ONE DEGREE LESS THAN YOU DO NOW.

I MEAN TO OFFER SOME EXPLANATION, SOME KIND OF APOLOGY, TO OPEN MY HEART TO YOU. TO CONVINCE THAT WHILE I HAVE ALWAYS BEEN A BLOCKHEAD, I HAVE NOT ALWAYS BEEN A RASCAL.

TO OBTAIN SOMETHING LIKE FORGIVENESS FROM MAR--FROM YOUR SISTER.

YOU MAY BE SATISFIED ALREADY. SHE HAS *LONG* FORGIVEN YOU.

HAS SHE? THEN SHE SHALL AGAIN, ON MORE REASONABLE GROUNDS. *NOW* WILL YOU LISTEN TO ME?

I KNOW NOT WHAT DIABOLICAL MOTIVE YOU MIGHT HAVE IMPUTED TO ME IN MY TREATMENT OF YOUR SISTER, BUT WHEN I FIRST MET YOUR FAMILY, I HAD NO OTHER INTENTION THAN TO PASS THE TIME PLEASANTLY WHILE IN DEVON.

YOUR SISTER'S LOVELY PERSON AND MANNERS COULD NOT BUT PLEASE ME. HER BEHAVIOR TOWARD ME WAS SO SINGULAR. I ADMIT, AT FIRST, MY VANITY WAS ELEVATED BY IT.

I WAS CARELESS OF HER HAPPINESS, THINKING ONLY OF MY OWN AMUSEMENT.

I ENDEAVORED TO MAKE MYSELF PLEASING TO HER, WITHOUT ANY DESIGN OF RETURNING HER AFFECTION.

SUCH A BEGINNING CANNOT BE FOLLOWED BY ANYTHING. DO NOT LET ME BE PAINED BY HEARING ANY MORE ON THIS SUBJECT.

I INSIST ON YOU HEARING THE WHOLE OF IT.

MY FORTUNE WAS NOT LARGE, YET I HAD ALWAYS BEEN EXPENSIVE, EVERY YEAR INCREASING MY DEBTS. MRS. SMITH'S DEATH WAS TO SET ME FREE...YET THAT EVENT POSSIBLY BEING FAR DISTANT, I DETERMINED TO MARRY A WOMAN OF FORTUNE.

TO ATTACH MYSELF TO YOUR SISTER WAS NOT TO BE THOUGHT OF.

YET WITH A MEANNESS AND CRUELTY--WHICH NO INDIGNANT LOOK EVEN FROM YOU, MISS DASHWOOD, CAN EVER REPROBATE TOO MUCH--I SET OUT TO ENGAGE HER REGARD WITH NO THOUGHT OF RETURNING IT.

THE ONE THING THAT CAN BE SAID FOR ME IS THAT I DID NOT *THEN* KNOW WHAT IT WAS TO LOVE. HAD I EVER REALLY LOVED, COULD I SACRIFICE MY FEELINGS TO AVARICE OR VANITY?

BUT I HAVE DONE IT. TO AVOID A COMPARATIVE POVERTY, I HAVE, BY RAISING MYSELF TO AFFLUENCE, LOST EVERYTHING THAT COULD MAKE IT A BLESSING.

THEN YOU DID, AT ONE TIME, CONSIDER YOURSELF ATTACHED TO HER?

TO HAVE WITHSTOOD SUCH ATTRACTIONS, SUCH TENDERNESS? IS THERE A MAN ON EARTH WHO COULD HAVE DONE IT?

BUT EVEN AFTER I'D DETERMINED TO PAY MY ADDRESSES TO HER, I PUT IT OFF, TOO EMBARRASSED BY MY CIRCUMSTANCES TO ENTER INTO AN ENGAGEMENT.

THE DAY I RESOLVED TO MAKE IT RIGHT, MRS. SMITH WAS INFORMED BY A RELATION OF AN...AN AFFAIR, A CONNECTION OF MINE...I AM SURE YOU HAVE HEARD THE WHOLE STORY BY NOW.

I HAVE. AND HOW YOU WILL EXPLAIN AWAY YOUR GUILT IN THAT DREADFUL BUSINESS IS BEYOND COMPREHENSION.

AH, BECAUSE I AM THE LIBERTINE, SHE MUST BE A SAINT. YET CONSIDER THE VIOLENCE OF *HER* PASSIONS, THE WEAKNESS OF HER UNDERSTANDING.

I DO NOT MEAN TO DEFEND MYSELF...SHE DESERVED BETTER TREATMENT. YET COMMON SENSE OUGHT TO HAVE TOLD HER HOW TO FIND ME.

SO MRS. SMITH DISMISSED YOU FROM HER HOUSE.

BUT NOT FROM HER FAVOR, NOT IF I AGREED TO MARRY ELIZA. THAT COULD NOT BE, SO I WAS CAST OUT.

NOW YOU KNOW WHY I WAS SO DISTRAUGHT WHEN I LEFT YOU AT BARTON. I WILL NEVER FORGET MARIANNE'S SORROW, HER SADNESS.

WELL, SIR, AND THIS IS ALL?

YOU FORGET THAT INFAMOUS LETTER I WROTE HER. I GATHER SHE SHOWED IT TO YOU.

I SAW EVERY NOTE THAT PASSED BETWEEN YOU.

WHEN I LEARNED MARIANNE WAS IN TOWN, IT WAS A THUNDERBOLT. I THOUGHT OF HER EVERY MOMENT OF THE DAY.

IF YOU CAN *PITY* ME, PITY MY SITUATION AS IT WAS THEN, PAYING COURT TO ONE WOMAN, WITH MY HEAD AND HEART FULL OF YOUR SISTER.

AND THEN THE AGONY OF THAT PARTY... MARIANNE HOLDING OUT HER SWEET HAND TO ME ON ONE SIDE; SOPHIA, JEALOUS AS THE DEVIL ON THE OTHER.

YOUR SISTER WROTE TO ME THE NEXT MORNING...THE NOTE WAS BROUGHT TO ME WHILE I WAS BREAKFASTING WITH MISS GREY'S FAMILY.

WITH AN AIR OF PLAYFULNESS, SHE SEIZED AND OPENED IT. SHE WAS WRETCHED AFTERWARD, WHICH I COULD HAVE BORNE, BUT SHE WAS ALSO VENGEFUL.

SHE...SHE DICTATED MY RESPONSE TO YOUR SISTER. EVERY WORD.

BUT WHAT COULD I DO? WE WERE ENGAGED, EVERYTHING IN PREPARATION. SHE FORCED ME TO RETURN MARIANNE'S NOTES, HER DEAR LOCK OF HAIR.

EVERY MEMENTO WAS TORN FROM ME BY HER MALICE.

YOU OUGHT NOT SPEAK THAT WAY ABOUT MRS. WILLOUGHBY. YOU MADE YOUR CHOICE. SHE MUST BE ATTACHED TO YOU OR SHE WOULD NOT HAVE MARRIED YOU.

SHE KNEW I HAD NO REGARD FOR HER WHEN WE WED. YET WE ARE MEANT TO BE HAPPY AND GAY.

NOW DO YOU PITY ME, MISS DASHWOOD?

YOU HAVE PROVED YOURSELF LESS FAULTY, LESS WICKED, THAN I BELIEVED YOU. BUT THE MISERY YOU INFLICTED...

I HARDLY KNOW HOW YOU COULD HAVE MADE IT WORSE.

AND WILL YOU TELL MARIANNE, WHEN SHE IS RECOVERED? TELL HER OF MY PENITENCE, OF MY CONSTANCY, THAT AT THIS MOMENT SHE IS DEARER TO ME THAN EVER.

I WILL TELL HER WHAT IS NECESSARY, OF WHAT YOU CALL YOUR JUSTIFICATION.

WELL, GOODBYE. I SHALL GO NOW AND LIVE IN DREAD OF ONE EVENT.

WHAT DO YOU MEAN?

YOUR SISTER'S MARRIAGE.

SHE CAN NEVER BE MORE LOST TO YOU THAN SHE IS NOW.

BUT SHE WILL BE GAINED BY SOMEONE ELSE-- POSSIBLY BY THE ONE MAN I COULD LEAST BEAR.

I'M LEAVING NOW...I WILL NOT ROB MYSELF OF YOUR GOOD WILL BY SHOWING THAT WHERE I HAVE MOST INJURED, I CAN LEAST FORGIVE.

ELINOR SAT FOR A TIME, OPPRESSED BY A CROWD OF IDEAS.

FOR ALL HIS FAULTS, WILLOUGHBY HAS EXCITED IN ME A DEGREE OF COMMISERATION FOR THE SUFFERINGS PRODUCED BY THEM.

I THINK OF HIM NOW, FOREVER SEPARATED FROM OUR FAMILY, WITH TENDERNESS AND WITH REGRET.

I KNOW MYSELF TO BE INFLUENCED BY CIRCUMSTANCES WHICH OUGHT NOT IN REASON TO HAVE WEIGHT--HIS OPEN, AFFECTIONATE, AND LIVELY MANNER...AND HIS STILL ARDENT LOVE FOR MARIANNE.

I SHOULD NOT INDULGE IN THOSE FEELINGS, YET IT WILL BE MANY DAYS BEFORE HIS INFLUENCE FADES.

ELINOR'S MUSINGS WERE DISTURBED BY ANOTHER ARRIVAL.

BE EASY, DEAR MAMA. SHE IS WELL, SHE IS OUT OF DANGER.

I FEARED I HAD LOST YOU, MY MOST PRECIOUS GIRL.

I LONGED FOR YOU SO, MAMA. EVEN IN MY FEVERED DREAMS.

YOUR MAMA IS HERE NOW. THANKS TO COLONEL BRANDON.

COLONEL, YOUR KINDNESS TO OUR FAMILY IS BEYOND MEASURE. HOW SHALL WE EVER REPAY YOU?

YOUR COMPLETE RECOVERY IS ALL I ASK, MISS MARIANNE.

MRS. DASHWOOD SPENT THE NIGHT SITTING AT HER DAUGHTER'S BEDSIDE, THEN SOUGHT OUT ELINOR THE NEXT MORNING AFTER BREAKFAST.

MY ELINOR, YOU DO NOT YET KNOW ALL MY HAPPINESS. COLONEL BRANDON LOVES MARIANNE. HE TOLD ME SO HIMSELF DURING OUR JOURNEY. HIS REGARD FOR HER INFINITELY SURPASSES ANYTHING WILLOUGHBY FELT FOR HER.

YOU ARE NEVER LIKE ME, ELINOR, OR I SHOULD WONDER AT YOUR COMPOSURE NOW.

COLONEL BRANDON'S CHARACTER, AS AN EXCELLENT MAN, IS WELL ESTABLISHED. WHAT ANSWER DID YOU GIVE HIM... DID YOU ALLOW HIM TO HOPE?

I COULD NOT THEN TALK OF HOPE. MARIANNE MIGHT BE DYING FOR ALL WE KNEW. IT WAS NOT AN APPLICATION TO A PARENT, BUT AN INVOLUNTARY CONFIDENCE TO A FRIEND.

I DID TELL HIM THIS MORNING THAT I WILL GIVE HIM EVERY ENCOURAGEMENT IN MY POWER. TIME, I TOLD HIM, WILL DO EVERYTHING.

MARIANNE'S HEART IS NOT TO BE WASTED ON A MAN LIKE WILLOUGHBY-- BUT BRANDON'S OWN MERITS MUST SOON SECURE IT.

TO JUDGE FROM HIS SPIRITS AT BREAKFAST, YOU HAVE NOT MADE HIM VERY SANGUINE.

ALAS, HE THINKS MARIANNE'S AFFECTIONS TOO DEEPLY ROOTED. AND WERE SHE EVER FREE, HE FEARS THAT WITH SUCH A DIFFERENCE IN THEIR AGE AND DISPOSITION, HE COULD NEVER ATTACH HER. YET I AM WELL CONVINCED HE IS THE VERY ONE TO MAKE HER HAPPY.

HIS GENTLENESS, HIS GENUINE ATTENTION TO OTHER PEOPLE, AND THE MANLY UNSTUDIED SIMPLICITY OF HIS MANNER IS MUCH MORE ACCORDANT WITH HER REAL DISPOSITION, THAN THE LIVELINESS--OFTEN ARTIFICIAL AND ILL-TIMED--OF THE OTHER.

AT DELAFORD, SHE WILL BE AN EASY DISTANCE FROM ME.

ONCE THEY ARE SETTLED, I AM SURE WE COULD FIND A COTTAGE SIMILAR TO BARTON NEARBY.

OH, DEAR, HERE IS YET ANOTHER SCHEME TO GET ME TO DELAFORD!

WITHIN A WEEK'S TIME, MARIANNE WAS WELL ENOUGH TO RETURN HOME. COLONEL BRANDON OFFERED THE USE OF HIS CARRIAGE TO MAKE HER JOURNEY MORE COMFORTABLE.

I WILL COME BY BARTON TO REDEEM THE CARRIAGE IN A FEW WEEKS' TIME.

WE SHALL LOOK FORWARD TO SEEING YOU, COLONEL.

ELINOR OBSERVED HER SISTER'S PLEASURE ON THE JOURNEY HOME WITH RELIEF. BUT AS THEY NEARED BARTON...

I'M SORRY...I TRULY DON'T WANT TO MAKE A FUSS.

NO, IT'S ONLY NATURAL.

I...I HAVE BEEN THINKING. WHEN I HAVE RECOVERED MY STRENGTH, WE WILL TAKE LONG WALKS TOGETHER EVERY DAY. TO THE FARM, TO BARTON PARK TO SEE THE CHILDREN. I KNOW THE SUMMER WILL PASS HAPPILY AWAY. I MEAN TO RISE NO LATER THAN SIX AND SHALL DEVOTE EVERY MOMENT TO READING AND MUSIC.

I HAVE DETERMINED TO APPLY MYSELF TO SERIOUS STUDY. THERE ARE MANY WORKS WORTH READING AT THE PARK, AND OTHERS OF MORE MODERN PRODUCTION, I CAN BORROW FROM COLONEL BRANDON. I SHALL GAIN IN THE COURSE OF TWELVE-MONTHS A GREAT DEAL OF INSTRUCTION WHICH I NOW FEEL MYSELF TO LACK.

A VERY NOBLE PLAN.

THE SAME EAGER FANCY THAT LED HER TO AN EXTREME OF LANGUID REPINING AND SELFISH INDOLENCE IS NOW AT WORK INTRODUCING EXCESS INTO A SCHEME OF RATIONAL EMPLOYMENT AND VIRTUOUS SELF CONTROL.

I KNOW I PROMISED WILLOUGHBY TO TELL HER OF HIS VISIT, BUT I WILL WAIT UNTIL HER HEALTH IS MORE SECURE.

BUT THE RESOLUTION WAS MADE ONLY TO BE BROKEN.

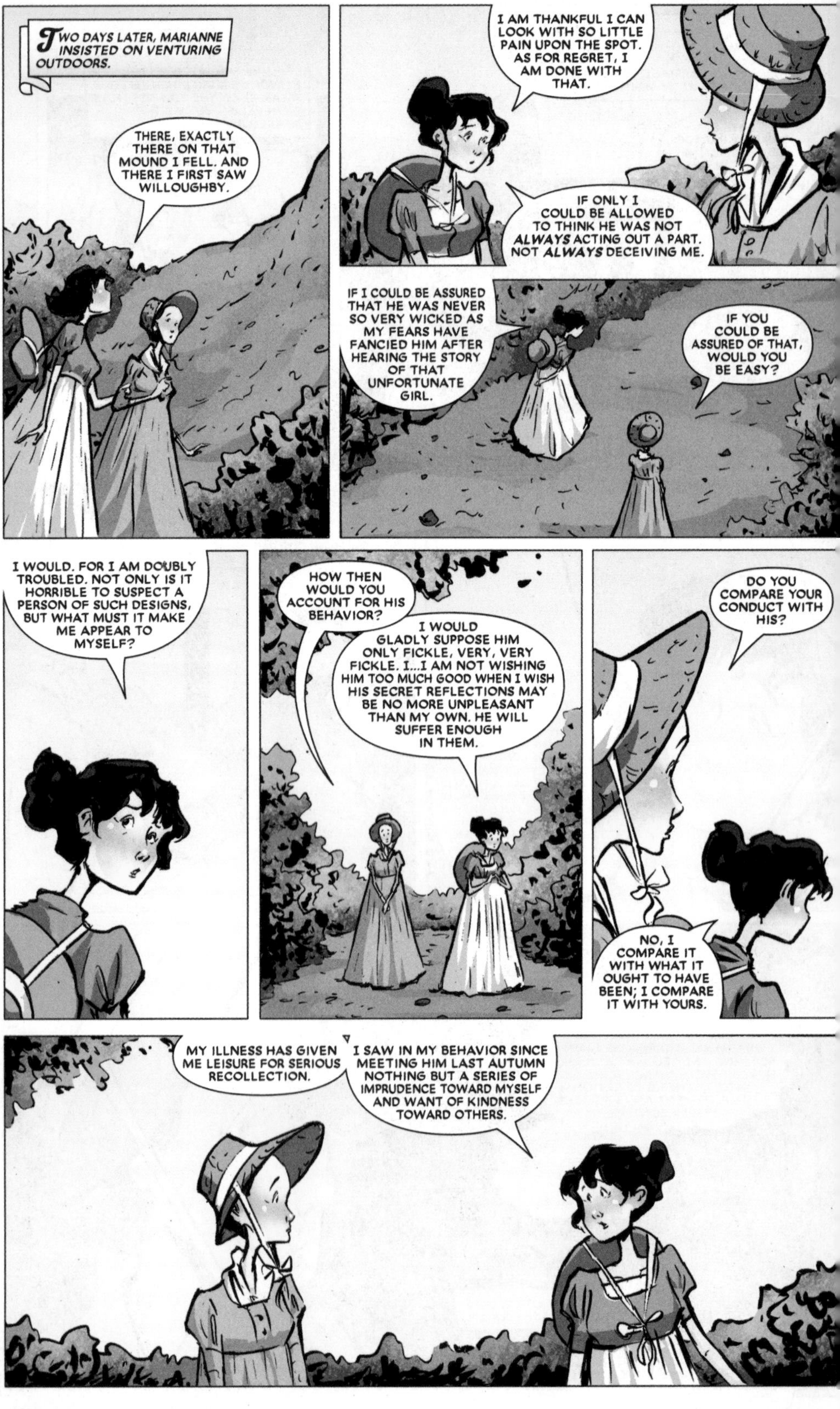
TWO DAYS LATER, MARIANNE INSISTED ON VENTURING OUTDOORS.
THERE, EXACTLY THERE ON THAT MOUND I FELL. AND THERE I FIRST SAW WILLOUGHBY.
I AM THANKFUL I CAN LOOK WITH SO LITTLE PAIN UPON THE SPOT. AS FOR REGRET, I AM DONE WITH THAT.
IF ONLY I COULD BE ALLOWED TO THINK HE WAS NOT *ALWAYS* ACTING OUT A PART. NOT *ALWAYS* DECEIVING ME.
IF I COULD BE ASSURED THAT HE WAS NEVER SO VERY WICKED AS MY FEARS HAVE FANCIED HIM AFTER HEARING THE STORY OF THAT UNFORTUNATE GIRL.
IF YOU COULD BE ASSURED OF THAT, WOULD YOU BE EASY?
I WOULD. FOR I AM DOUBLY TROUBLED. NOT ONLY IS IT HORRIBLE TO SUSPECT A PERSON OF SUCH DESIGNS, BUT WHAT MUST IT MAKE ME APPEAR TO MYSELF?
HOW THEN WOULD YOU ACCOUNT FOR HIS BEHAVIOR?
I WOULD GLADLY SUPPOSE HIM ONLY FICKLE, VERY, VERY FICKLE. I...I AM NOT WISHING HIM TOO MUCH GOOD WHEN I WISH HIS SECRET REFLECTIONS MAY BE NO MORE UNPLEASANT THAN MY OWN. HE WILL SUFFER ENOUGH IN THEM.
DO YOU COMPARE YOUR CONDUCT WITH HIS?
NO, I COMPARE IT WITH WHAT IT OUGHT TO HAVE BEEN; I COMPARE IT WITH YOURS.
MY ILLNESS HAS GIVEN ME LEISURE FOR SERIOUS RECOLLECTION.
I SAW IN MY BEHAVIOR SINCE MEETING HIM LAST AUTUMN NOTHING BUT A SERIES OF IMPRUDENCE TOWARD MYSELF AND WANT OF KINDNESS TOWARD OTHERS.

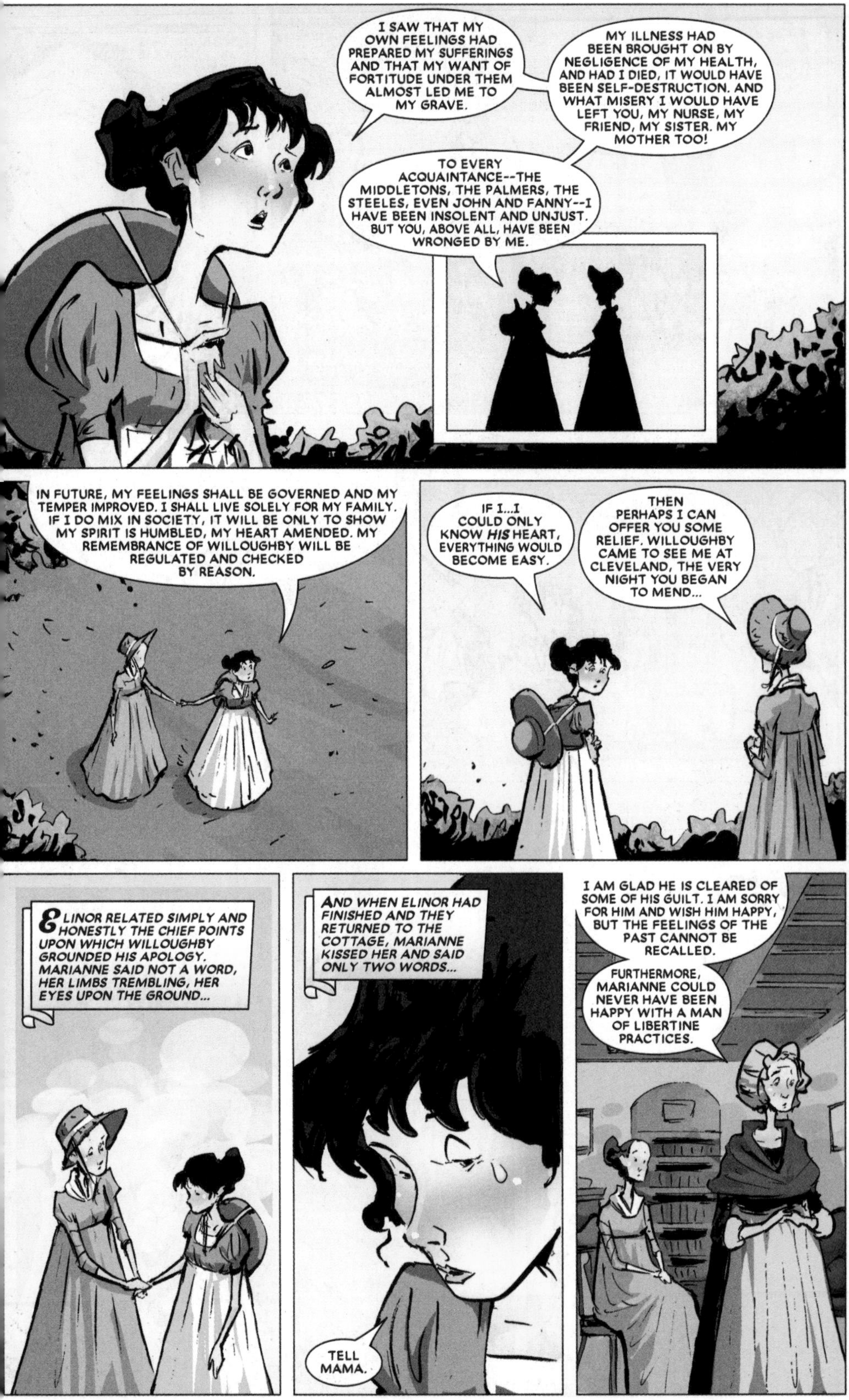
I SAW THAT MY OWN FEELINGS HAD PREPARED MY SUFFERINGS AND THAT MY WANT OF FORTITUDE UNDER THEM ALMOST LED ME TO MY GRAVE.
MY ILLNESS HAD BEEN BROUGHT ON BY NEGLIGENCE OF MY HEALTH, AND HAD I DIED, IT WOULD HAVE BEEN SELF-DESTRUCTION. AND WHAT MISERY I WOULD HAVE LEFT YOU, MY NURSE, MY FRIEND, MY SISTER. MY MOTHER TOO!
TO EVERY ACQUAINTANCE--THE MIDDLETONS, THE PALMERS, THE STEELES, EVEN JOHN AND FANNY--I HAVE BEEN INSOLENT AND UNJUST. BUT YOU, ABOVE ALL, HAVE BEEN WRONGED BY ME.
IN FUTURE, MY FEELINGS SHALL BE GOVERNED AND MY TEMPER IMPROVED. I SHALL LIVE SOLELY FOR MY FAMILY. IF I DO MIX IN SOCIETY, IT WILL BE ONLY TO SHOW MY SPIRIT IS HUMBLED, MY HEART AMENDED. MY REMEMBRANCE OF WILLOUGHBY WILL BE REGULATED AND CHECKED BY REASON.
IF I...I COULD ONLY KNOW *HIS* HEART, EVERYTHING WOULD BECOME EASY.
THEN PERHAPS I CAN OFFER YOU SOME RELIEF. WILLOUGHBY CAME TO SEE ME AT CLEVELAND, THE VERY NIGHT YOU BEGAN TO MEND...
ELINOR RELATED SIMPLY AND HONESTLY THE CHIEF POINTS UPON WHICH WILLOUGHBY GROUNDED HIS APOLOGY. MARIANNE SAID NOT A WORD, HER LIMBS TREMBLING, HER EYES UPON THE GROUND...
AND WHEN ELINOR HAD FINISHED AND THEY RETURNED TO THE COTTAGE, MARIANNE KISSED HER AND SAID ONLY TWO WORDS...
TELL MAMA.
I AM GLAD HE IS CLEARED OF SOME OF HIS GUILT. I AM SORRY FOR HIM AND WISH HIM HAPPY, BUT THE FEELINGS OF THE PAST CANNOT BE RECALLED.
FURTHERMORE, MARIANNE COULD NEVER HAVE BEEN HAPPY WITH A MAN OF LIBERTINE PRACTICES.

THE FAMILY'S PEACE WAS AT LEAST RESTORED AND LIFE RETURNED TO NORMAL AT THE COTTAGE. UNTIL THE MORNING A SERVANT WAS SENT ON SOME BUSINESS TO EXETER:

I SUPPOSE YOU KNOW THAT MR. FERRARS IS MARRIED.

MARRIED!

MISS MARIANNE!

I'LL SEE TO MARIANNE, THOMAS. WHO TOLD YOU THAT MR. FERRARS WAS MARRIED?

I SAW MR. FERRARS MYSELF. THIS MORNING IN EXETER, AND HIS LADY TOO. AS WAS MISS STEELE. SHE KNEW ME AND CALLED ME OVER TO THEIR CARRIAGE. SENT HER COMPLIMENTS TO THIS HOUSE.

BUT DID SHE TELL YOU SHE WAS MARRIED?

SHE SMILED AND SAID HOW SHE HAD CHANGED HER NAME SINCE SHE WAS LAST IN THESE PARTS. MR. FERRARS WAS IN THE CARRIAGE, LEANING BACK, BUT HE DID NOT LOOK UP.

THANK YOU, THOMAS, THAT WILL BE ALL.

I DON'T BELIEVE I CAN FINISH MY SUPPER.

I'M AFRAID WE'VE ALL LOST OUR APPETITE.

ELINOR NOW EXPERIENCED THE DIFFERENCE BETWEEN THE EXPECTATION OF AN UNPLEASANT EVENT AND CERTAINTY ITSELF.

I HAVE TO ADMIT I CARRIED WITH ME A HOPE THAT WHILE HE REMAINED SINGLE, SOMETHING MIGHT OCCUR TO PREVENT HIM FROM MARRYING LUCY. AND NOW IT'S HAPPENED, AND MUCH SOONER THAN I EXPECTED. NO DOUBT LUCY HASTENED THINGS ALONG, OVERLOOKING EVERYTHING BUT THE RISK OF DELAY.

A FEW DAYS LATER...

THERE'S A RIDER COMING UP THE LANE. ARE WE EXPECTING COLONEL BRANDON?

HE COULD ARRIVE AT ANY TIME, ACCORDING TO HIS LAST LETTER.

IT'S NOT THE COLONEL. IT'S EDWARD.

GOOD HEAVENS!

EDWARD, DEAR BOY, LET ME WISH YOU GREAT JOY.

I...ER, THAT IS...AH... THANK YOU.

COME AND SIT...I TRUST MRS. FERRARS IS WELL.

MY MOTHER WAS QUITE WELL THE LAST TIME I SAW HER IN LONDON.

I BELIEVE MY MOTHER MEANT TO INQUIRE FOR MRS. *EDWARD* FERRARS.

PERHAPS YOU MEAN MY BROTHER'S WIFE, MRS. *ROBERT* FERRARS.

MRS. ROBERT FERRARS!

PERHAPS YOU DO NOT KNOW, HAVE NOT HEARD THAT MY BROTHER IS LATELY MARRIED TO THE YOUNGEST MISS STEELE. LUCY STEELE.

AH-AH-AH...

ELINOR, OVERCOME BY EMOTION, FLED THE ROOM. EDWARD QUICKLY FOLLOWED.

ELINOR, MY ONLY ERRAND AT BARTON TODAY WAS A SIMPLE ONE. TO ASK YOU TO MARRY ME.

CONSIDERING I AM NOT ALTOGETHER INEXPERIENCED AT SUCH A QUESTION, I WONDER THAT I FEEL SO UNCOMFORTABLE IN THE PRESENT CASE.

I...I FIND MYSELF IN NEED OF ENCOURAGEMENT AND FRESH AIR.

WILL YOU WALK WITH ME?

YES, MOST HAPPILY.

SO YOU HEARD THAT LUCY STEELE HAD MARRIED MR. FERRARS AND ASSUMED IT WAS ME?

WHY SHOULD WE HAVE THOUGHT OTHERWISE? WHEN I MET YOUR BROTHER AT HARLEY STREET, HE WAS HARDLY COMPLIMENTARY TO LUCY.

THAT WAS EXACTLY LIKE ROBERT. *THAT* MIGHT HAVE BEEN IN HIS HEAD WHEN FIRST THEY MET. AND LUCY AT FIRST MIGHT HAVE THOUGHT ONLY OF PROCURING HIS GOOD OFFICES IN MY FAVOR. OTHER DESIGNS MIGHT AFTERWARD HAVE ARISEN.

YOU COULD SUPPOSE THAT THE VANITY OF ONE HAD BEEN SO WORKED ON BY THE FLATTERY OF THE OTHER...AND LEAD BY DEGREES TO ALL ELSE. AND YET YOU HAD NO SUSPICION?

NOT UNTIL I RECEIVED A LETTER FROM HER. I WAS HALF STUPEFIED BY THE WONDER, THE HORROR, AND THE JOY AT SUCH A DELIVERANCE.

I HAVE LONG WONDERED HOW I CAME TO ASK HER TO WED. I SUSPECT IT WAS A FOOLISH, IDLE INCLINATION ON MY SIDE. IF I HAD ENTERED OXFORD DIRECTLY, I WOULD HAVE BEEN DISTRACTED. INSTEAD, I SPENT A YEAR WITH NO OCCUPATION, FANCYING MYSELF IN LOVE.

ROBERT IS NOW SIMILARLY AFFLICTED. AND HOWEVER THE CONNECTION BETWEEN LUCY AND YOUR BROTHER MAY HAVE COME ABOUT, THEY ARE CERTAINLY MARRIED. YOUR MOTHER HAS BROUGHT UPON HERSELF A MOST APPROPRIATE PUNISHMENT-- THE INDEPENDENCE SHE SETTLED ON ROBERT TO SPITE YOU, GAVE ONE SON THE POWER TO MAKE HIS OWN CHOICE, ALLOWING HIM TO DO THE VERY DEED SHE DISINHERITED THE OTHER FOR INTENDING TO DO.

SHE WILL BE MORE HURT BY ROBERT'S ACTIONS. HE WAS ALWAYS HER FAVORITE. AND ON THE SAME PRINCIPLE WILL FORGIVE HIM THE SOONER. WHAT I CANNOT FATHOM IS WHY LUCY INSISTED ON GOING FORWARD WITH OUR ENGAGEMENT ONCE I LOST MY INHERITANCE.

I IMAGINE THE CONNECTION GAVE HER STATURE AMONG HER FRIENDS. AND SHE HAS PROVED THAT THE ENGAGEMENT FETTERED NEITHER HER INCLINATIONS NOR HER ACTIONS.

THOUGH YOU ARE NOT BLAMELESS. YOU MUST HAVE FELT YOUR OWN INCONSTANCY WHILE YOU ARE AT NORLAND. TO SAY NOTHING OF MY OWN CONVICTION, MY RELATIONS WERE ALL LED TO FANCY AND EXPECT *WHAT*, AS YOU WERE *THEN* SITUATED, COULD NEVER BE.

I DID NOT BELIEVE THERE COULD BE ANY DANGER IN MY BEING WITH YOU. I ADMIRED YOU, BUT TOLD MYSELF IT WAS FRIENDSHIP I FELT. I CAN ONLY PLEAD IGNORANCE OF MY OWN HEART.

AND NOW?

NOW I HAD BETTER RETURN TO THE COTTAGE AND ASK YOUR MOTHER PROPERLY FOR YOUR HAND.

WHEN THE FAMILY SAT DOWN TO SUPPER THAT NIGHT, EDWARD HAD SECURED HIS LADY, ENGAGED HER MOTHER'S CONSENT, AND WAS IN THE RAPTUROUS PROFESSION OF THE LOVER.

INDEED, HIS RELEASE FROM LUCY--A WOMAN HE HAD LONG CEASED TO LOVE--ELEVATED HIM FROM MISERY TO HAPPINESS AND BROUGHT ABOUT A GENUINE, FLOWING CHEERFULNESS HIS FRIENDS HAD NEVER BEFORE WITNESSED.

FOUR DAYS AFTER EDWARD'S ARRIVAL, COLONEL BRANDON APPEARED. MRS. DASHWOOD FINALLY HAD THE SATISFACTION OF RECEIVING MORE GUESTS THAN HER COTTAGE WOULD HOLD.

I'LL GLADLY GIVE EDWARD THE PRIVILEGE OF FIRST COMER. I CAN RETURN TO MY OLD QUARTERS AT THE PARK EACH NIGHT.

THE TWO GENTLEMEN ADVANCED IN THEIR GOOD OPINION OF EACH OTHER. THEIR BEING IN LOVE WITH TWO SISTERS, AND TWO SISTERS FOND OF EACH OTHER, MADE THAT MUTUAL REGARD INEVITABLE AND IMMEDIATE.

THAT AUTUMN, ELINOR AND EDWARD WERE MARRIED IN BARTON CHURCH.

AFTER A PROPER PERIOD OF RESISTANCE, MRS. FERRARS ADMITTED EDWARD TO HER PRESENCE AND AGAIN PRONOUNCED HIM HER SON. SHE DID COME TO VISIT THEM AT THE PARSONAGE, AND ALWAYS TREATED THEM WITH THE MAKE BELIEVE OF DECENT AFFECTION, BUT THEY WERE NEVER INSULTED BY HER REAL FAVOR.

THIS WAS DUE TO THE CUNNING OF LUCY, WHOSE ENDLESS FLATTERIES OF MRS. FERRARS SOON RE-ESTABLISHED ROBERT AS THE FAVORITE SON.

THIS IS BY FAR THE MOST COMFORTABLE SEAT IN THE PARLOR, DEAREST MAMA.

FANNY AND JOHN DASHWOOD CONTINUED TO MAKE DUE, SCRAPING BY WITH WHAT THEY CONSIDERED TO BE A MEAGER INCOME.

THE PROPOSED ORANGERY AT NORLAND IS MUCH TOO SMALL. IT WILL BARELY HOLD A DOZEN GUESTS.

MARIANNE, BORN TO DISCOVER THE FALSEHOOD OF HER OWN OPINIONS, SOON FOUND HERSELF SUBMITTING TO NEW ATTACHMENTS AND ENTERING ON NEW DUTIES--AS A WIFE, MISTRESS OF A NEW HOME, AND THE PATRONESS OF A VILLAGE.

IN MARIANNE, COLONEL BRANDON WAS CONSOLED FOR EVERY PAST AFFLICTION.

WILLOUGHBY HEARD OF HER MARRIAGE WITH A PANG OF REGRET. NOT LONG AFTER, MRS. SMITH FORGAVE HIM, NAMING HIS MARRIAGE TO A WOMAN OF CHARACTER AS THE SOURCE OF HER CLEMENCY.

HE REALIZED THEN THAT HE COULD HAVE WED MARIANNE AND BEEN BOTH HAPPY AND RICH.

MRS. DASHWOOD DID NOT MOVE IN WITH EITHER DAUGHTER, BUT WISELY REMAINED IN HER COTTAGE.

YET BETWEEN BARTON AND DELAFORD THERE WAS THAT CONSTANT COMMUNICATION WHICH FAMILY AFFECTION WOULD NATURALLY DICTATE.

THE END!

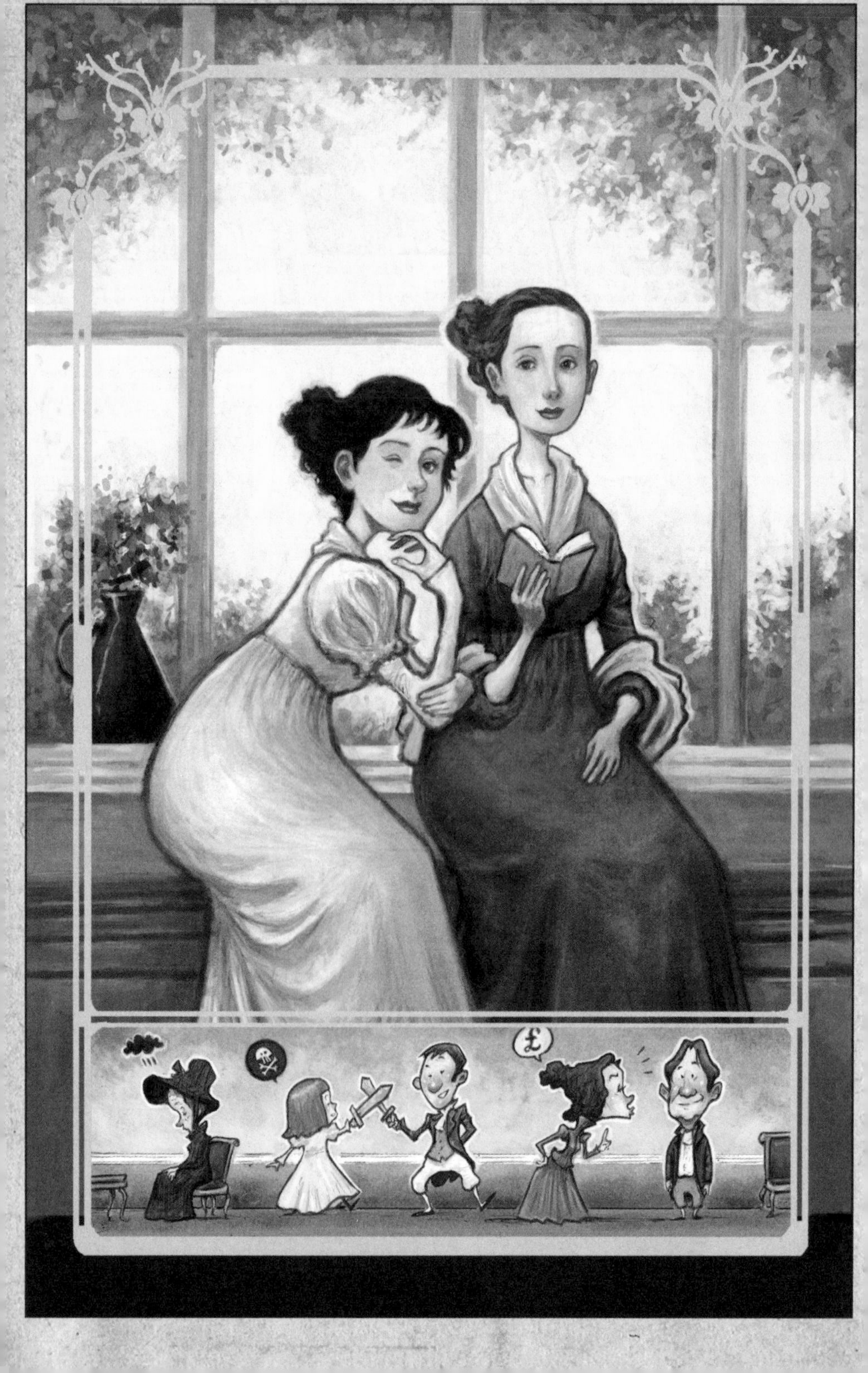
£

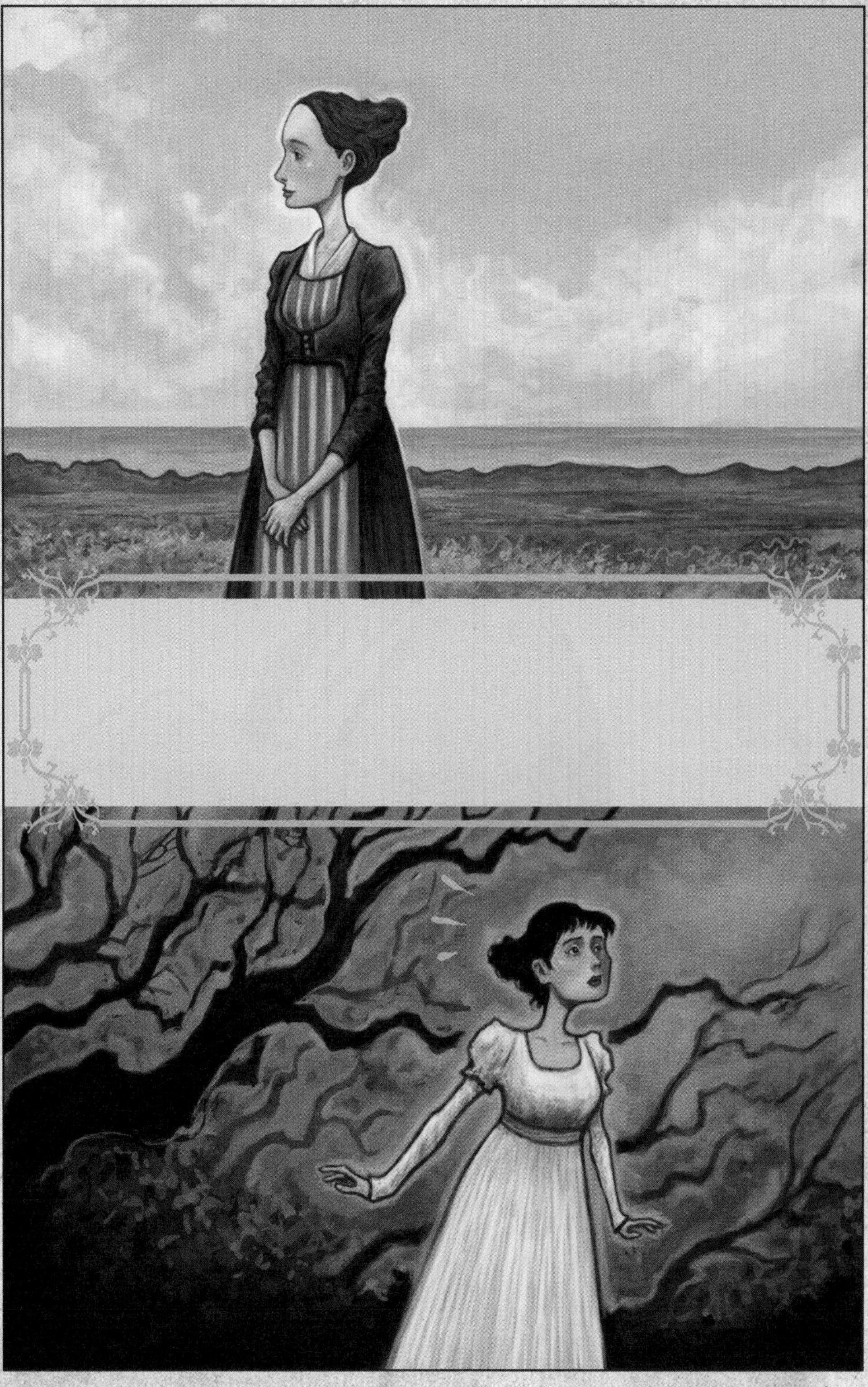

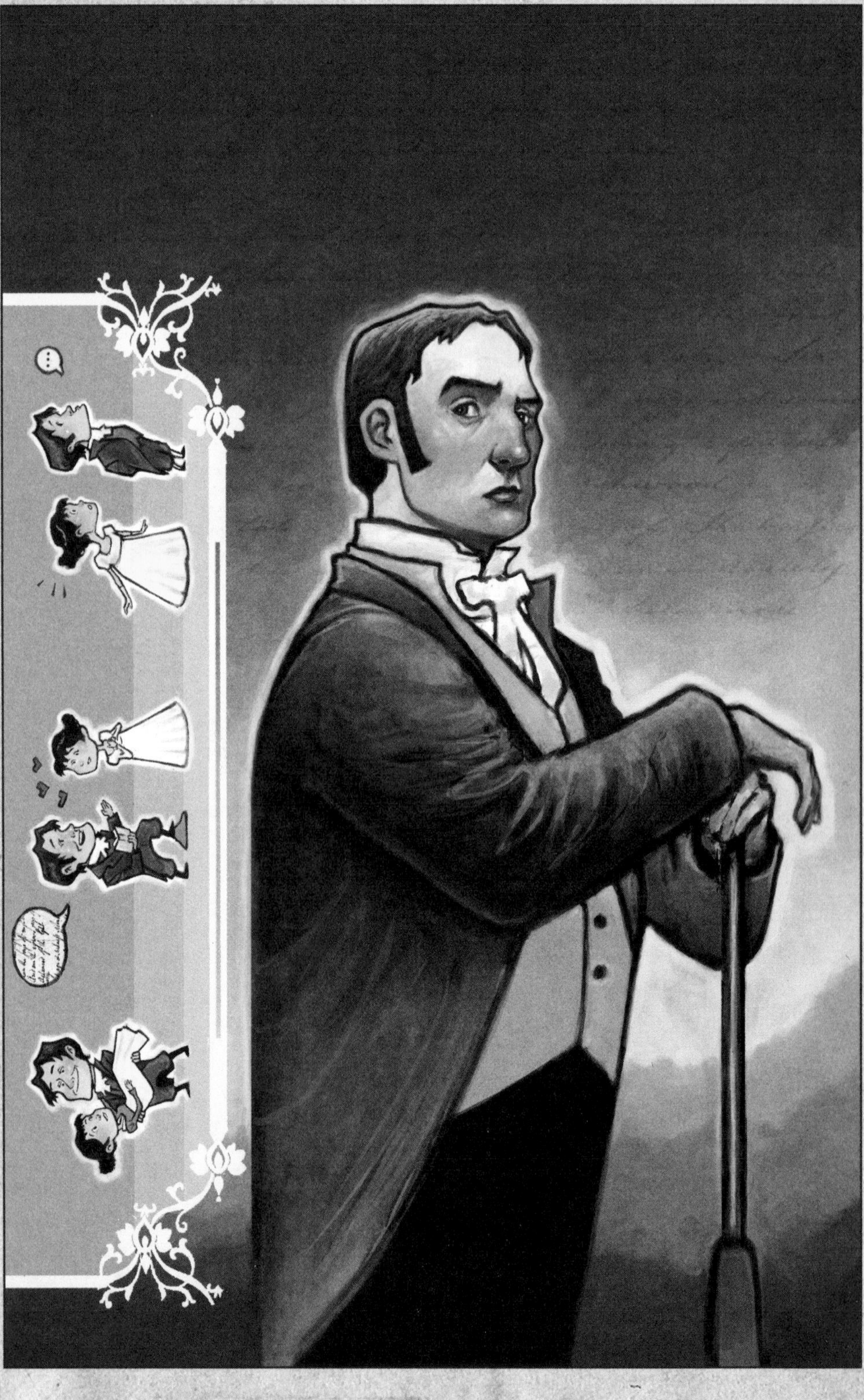